Jesus on Leadership—a must read for those who value their family. This book is most inspiring and practical. I'm pleased to recommend it.

WILLIAM MITCHELL, author of *Building Strong Families,* founder of Power of Positive Students

It was my opportunity to be led by God to enlist Gene Wilkes to write the curriculum edition of *Jesus on Leadership: Becoming a Servant Leader* for LifeWay Press. Gene's message communicates the biblical servant leadership demonstrated by Jesus and has helped equip church leaders to be more effective. In the same way, I believe this tailored Tyndale House edition will have incredible impact on leaders in business, industry, government, and schools, as well as churches. This edition of *Jesus on Leadership* is simply proof of how God's energizing presence has brought together spiritual gifts, experiences, relating style, and vocational skills in Gene Wilkes's life to serve all leaders who desire their lives to please and serve God. The quality of what Gene has done is an example of how God can and does develop a person's capacity to understand and apply God's servant leadership principles in the daily walk of life. For God's touch on Gene's mind and heart in the writing of *Jesus on Leadership,* I say, "Thank you, God!"

HENRY WEBB, director, Discipleship and Family Leadership Department, publisher of LifeWay Edition of *Jesus on Leadership: Becoming a Servant Leader*

Read at your own risk. Gene Wilkes may change your whole view of leadership. While *Jesus on Leadership* is a practical tool kit, Wilkes's unusual writing gifts make it stirring devotional reading as well. And it is no book of theory. This material flows from the heart and hands of an authentic servant leader. Besides living these principles himself, Gene Wilkes has trained and mentored scores of leaders, Jesus-style. I am delighted that he has now spelled out his heart in print for the benefit of thousands. This refreshing book deserves top priority on the reading list of every Christian. I predict it will be around for a long time.

LYNN ANDERSON, president, Hope Network Ministries, author of *They Smell Like Sheep: Biblical Leadership for the Twenty-First Century*

Spiritual formation is the biggest issue for leaders in the church. The need is obvious, most notably demonstrated by the lack of genuine spiritual vibrancy in so many who occupy positions of influence among Christian congregations and institutions. Help has now arrived! What Gene Wilkes says is right on target at delivering a corrective for so much of what we see masquerading as Christian leadership. Don't read this book if you are unwilling to be challenged—or even changed!

REGGIE MCNEAL, director of leadership development, South Carolina Baptist Convention

Gene Wilkes's description of leadership according to Jesus—"I am a mission and I serve those who are on that mission"—has captured the heart and passion of the mission-driven leader.

BILL EASUM, author of *Growing Spiritual Redwoods* and director of 21st Century Strategies

I have known Gene Wilkes since he was eighteen. He has lived his life as a servant leader. This has been his passion. The insights I have received from reading this book will forever change the way I do my job and live my life.

GARY COOK, president, Dallas Baptist University

Gene Wilkes, my friend and fellow pastor, serves us lessons on leadership that have been simmering for a lifetime. Centered around the meat of Christ's ministry, they are complemented by wise counsel for others and flavored with experience. Although the truth is often hard to swallow, Gene's recipe for servant leadership is both delicious and nutritious. It's a feast fit for a King, coach, pastor, or parent. Enjoy!

GENE A. GETZ, author of *The Measure of a Man,* senior pastor, Fellowship Bible Church North, Richardson, Texas

JESUS ON LEADERSHIP

ON JESUS LEADERSHIP

C. GENE WILKES, Ph.D.

 TYNDALE HOUSE PUBLISHERS, INC.
WHEATON, ILLINOIS

Visit Tyndale's exciting Web site at www.tyndale.com

Edited by Vinita Hampton Wright

Designed by Julie Chen

Library of Congress Cataloging-in-Publication Data

Wilkes, C. Gene
  Jesus on leadership / C. Gene Wilkes
    p.   cm.
  Includes bibliographical references.
  ISBN 0-8423-1863-1 (sc : alk. paper)
    1. Leadership—Religious aspects—Christianity. 2. Jesus Christ—
Leadership. I. Title.
BV4597.53.L43W55 1998
253—dc21   98-24160

Printed in the United States of America

06 05 04 03 02 01
10 9 8 7 6 5

CONTENTS

FOREWORD

THERE are some books the world waits for without ever knowing it is waiting. *Jesus on Leadership* is such a book. When such books are written, they inevitably can have no more than one source. There is not a guild of authors for the books that must be written and must be read.

For some time now I have known that Gene Wilkes was working on this book. I have prayed for him throughout this long season of his dedication. I have seen him emerge from his cocoon of creativity before. Behind him, through the doorway of his study, can be seen the titles of hundreds of different books that have been his companions and future for his mental sojourn. But the fact that Gene Wilkes knows the literature of leadership is not why this book is the finest of its kind in the marketplace.

There are four major contributors to Gene Wilkes's greatness as a scholar and teacher. These same four forces permeate this book and make it a must for all of those who want to become informed and capable leaders.

First, Gene Wilkes loves Jesus. Please don't think this a

mere saccharine appraisal between friends. This simplicity provides Gene his passion to serve both God and his congregation. Further, this love for Christ carries a subtle and pervasive authenticity that makes Gene Wilkes believable. Whether you read him or hear him lecture, you walk away from the experience knowing that what you've heard is the truth—the life-changing truth from a man who lives the truth and loves getting to the bottom of things. All this I believe derives from his love of Christ.

Second, Gene is a practitioner of servant leadership. When he encourages you to pick up the basin and towel and wash feet, you may be sure it is not empty theory. He teaches others what he has learned in the laboratory of his own experience. Gene is a servant leader, and even as he wrote this book, he directed his very large church through a massive building program. His church leadership ability, which he exhibited during this writing project, does not surface in this volume, but it undergirds and authenticates it.

Third, Gene Wilkes knows better than anyone else the literature of leadership. As you read this book, you will quickly feel his command of his subject. Footnotes will come and go, and behind the thin lines of numbers, ibids, and the like you will feel the force of his understanding. No one knows the field of both secular and Christian leadership like this man. So *Jesus on Leadership* is a mature essay. It has come from the only man I know with this vast comprehension of the subject.

Finally, Gene Wilkes is a born writer. It is not often that good oral communicators are good with the pen. But throughout this book, you will find the paragraphs coming and going so smoothly that you will be hard pressed to remember you are reading a definitive and scholarly work. Books that are this critically important should not be so much fun. Gene Wilkes is to leadership what Barbara Tuchman is to history. You know it's good for you and are surprised to be so delighted at taking the strong medicine that makes the world better.

All in all, there is joy throughout the realm of leadership. The waiting is over. Let the reading begin.

Calvin Miller
Fort Worth, Texas
April 1998

ACKNOWLEDGMENTS

THIS book is my confession that God is truly a gracious God. Only divine goodness, not my abilities or desires, has ultimately put this book in your hands.

My greatest thanks go to the people who are Legacy Drive Baptist Church. They have patiently waited for me to learn to lead. Their kindness, encouragement, and love for me and my family have made my first ten years as a pastor purposeful and fulfilling. I will be indebted to them for years to come.

My heartfelt thanks go to Henry Webb, who came to me with the idea of developing the Jesus on Leadership workbook. His friendship and trust in me allowed me to believe this book was possible.

Thanks, too, to Ralph Hodge, the "Man Who Was Thursday" in my life.

To John Kramp, author, friend, and leader, who believes in me and has been a "Barnabas" to me.

To Ron Beers and the team at Tyndale, who trusted me to write this book.

To Vinita Wright, my editor, who patiently mentored me through the process of producing a readable manuscript. Her fingerprints are all over this book.

To Calvin Miller, my hero, who has become a friend.

To my wife and best friend, Kim, who is the real servant leader in our family. And to my daughters, who make me accountable for everything I have held up as true in this book.

To my father, who models a servant's heart, and to my mother, who gave me a love of books and the dream to write one. And to my wife's parents, who have supported me as though I were their own son.

A CALL TO SERVANT LEADERSHIP

ALL true work combines [the] two elements of serving and ruling. Ruling is what we do; serving is how we do it. There's true sovereignty in all good work. There's no way to exercise it rightly other than by serving.
EUGENE PETERSON *Leap over a Wall*

ABOVE all, leadership is a position of servanthood.
MAX DEPREE *Leadership Jazz*

THE principle of service is what separates true leaders from glory seekers.
LAURIE BETH JONES *Jesus, CEO*

PEOPLE are supposed to serve. Life is a mission, not a career.
STEPHEN R. COVEY *The Leader of the Future*

ULTIMATELY the choice we make is between service and self-interest.
PETER BLOCK *Stewardship, Choosing Service over Self-Interest*

EVERYONE who exalts himself will be humbled, and he who humbles himself will be exalted.
JESUS *Luke 14:11*

I WILL never forget the second Tuesday evening of February 1996. We at Legacy Drive Baptist Church had struggled to retool ourselves to carry out the mission God had placed on our church: to make disciples who know Christ, share Christ, and multiply Christ in the life of another. During the transition, several core members left, attendance and giving went down, and the current church leadership—and I—began to question my ability to lead.

That evening, five men who loved God, our church, and me told me they had lost confidence in me as a leader. After meeting several times without my knowledge, these deacon officers had concluded that I was not the person for the next level of growth in the life of our church. They said it was not in their power or purpose to fire me, and they did not want to bring the issue to a vote because they knew it would split the church. Their job was to oversee the church and maintain its unity, not tear it apart. They asked me to take two weeks to pray and consider their position. They wanted to know my answer at the end of those two weeks.

As I walked from the house that evening, a strange sense of exhilaration came over me. These guys had done me a favor. They had put on the table what we all knew. I had stopped leading, and the church was floundering because of my lack of leadership. It was not long, however, before the elation turned to fear. I asked selfishly, "Why would God allow such a thing to happen to me?" Interestingly, just one month before, God had confirmed my call to and his vision for Legacy Drive. Ronnie and Tina Young, members of our church, had given me a trip to Robert Schuller's Institute of Successful Church Leadership as a Christmas gift. I went alone to recuperate and write. God began to confirm his vision in my heart as I heard Dr. Schuller say that prayers he had been praying for forty years were just then being answered. I listened as this misunderstood servant leader told how he had followed God to a unique mission field and had labored for forty years to see the call of God on his life completed.

I felt silly with my troubles, having been in my mission field for only nine years!

On the third day of the conference, Dr. Schuller said, "I don't know who you are, but a dozen, maybe thirty [out of about 1500]; but God just planted a seed of a dream in your heart. I want to pray for you." As Dr. Schuller prayed, I wept. I prayed, *God, help me.* It was not a prayer of desperation but a prayer for God to help me complete the task he had assigned for me to do at Legacy Drive and with my life. I wrote in my journal that day, "I prayed not out of fear but out of a great sense that God does want to do something with my life that I truly cannot do on my own. It was a prayer of release to let God work however he would choose. It was a prayer of confidence that God is love and answers prayer. I will be obedient to his call—that's what that prayer was about."

God had confirmed his call on my life in January. In February, God turned up the heat to test and change my heart.

The Sunday following the meeting with the deacon officers, I flew to Nashville to tape the training video to support the *Jesus on Leadership* workbook. When I landed, I asked Sam House, one of the project leaders, if they would still publish the work even if I were not a pastor. He didn't laugh. It was ironic that my denomination's publishing house was about to print a piece that I had written to help churches develop servant leaders—when I had just been told I wasn't leading!

As I was preparing to shoot the training videos Monday morning, I read through John 13 again. As clearly as I hear any voice, I heard God say, "Gene, I want you to wash their feet." I thought, *You've got to be kidding.* I read the story again. I sensed a moving of God's Spirit in my heart: *Wash the feet of those who have called you to this time of decision.* As we drove out to the shoot, I told Sam what God had said. He laughed this time and said, "Doesn't God have a sense of humor!"

After a day of shooting and an evening of recording the audio version of the workbook, I rode with Henry Webb and Ralph Hodge to Atlanta for the first Promise Keeper's Clergy Conference. While there, God changed my heart. One evening we heard Wellington Boone speak on reconciliation. He commented that while reconciliation between blacks and whites was important, God could not bring revival until blacks were reconciled among themselves. Wellington began to honor Tony Evans, a black pastor in Dallas. I did not know that Dr. Evans had been catching flack from the black community because he had reached out to whites.

Rev. Boone said in front of forty-two-thousand-plus clergy, "If I had a cup of water, I would wash Tony Evans's feet." The men of integrity would have nothing of idle words. Suddenly, a man jumped up and approached the stage with a glass of water. Almost immediately, another man came running down the aisle waving a towel. Men began to cheer and stand to their feet.

Another black clergyman on the platform, Bishop Porter, went to Tony Evans, stood him up, and led him to a chair on center stage. Wellington Boone took the towel and water, unlaced Evans's shoes, and washed his feet. The place erupted with emotion. Men began to cry at this display of humility and honor. I began to cry because I knew God really wanted me to wash the feet of those who had called me to decide how deep the mission of God was in my life. That was it. I knew. My responsibility was to wash their feet. God would take care of the rest.

I caught a plane back home before the conference was over. Jeff Koenigsberg, a twelve-year-old boy in our church family, had died of cancer while I was away. Jeff and my oldest daughter were the same age. I could not imagine the pain of his parents, Tom and Kris. The ordeal I faced was insignificant compared to what they had to endure. Washing feet is nothing compared to burying your son. Jeff's memorial service was Saturday. God used that event to calm my heart and remind me of the important things in life. On the flight home to Dallas, God had also graced my life by placing me beside Bob Dean, a friend from college, who listened to my story and encouraged me to do what God had told me to do. He had his own stories of servant leadership.

That Sunday I preached three morning services, attended team meetings in the afternoon, and preached a service that evening. The officers and I met in the church offices after the evening service. No one had approached me all day about our meeting two weeks earlier. They had done what they said they would do and waited to hear what I had to say.

When we all got into the room, I thanked them for drawing a line in the sand concerning my leadership and my commitment to the mission of God on our church. I told them there was one thing God had told me to do before I gave them my answer. I took a towel that I use to wipe the feet of those we set aside for service in our church, and I walked over to Ted, the chairman of deacons. I knelt before him and began to wipe the dust from his shoes. I began to weep. God had humbled my heart. I asked his forgiveness for not supporting him and allowing us to be drawn apart. I prayed for him as I did what God told me to do.

When I finished praying, I stood up. Ted stood, too. Talk about a pregnant pause. I had talked to none of the officers since my return. I didn't know if they had already put my termination package together or if they were really waiting to see what God had led me to do. Ted put his hands on my shoulders and turned me around to where he had been sitting. He took the towel from my hands and knelt before me. He, too, wiped my shoes and prayed for me. I could not hold back my emotions. I did not know what was next, but I now knew what reconciliation felt like.

After he finished, I returned to my chair. I told the group that God had confirmed my call to this church and its mission.

I sensed I was the one to lead in the days ahead. I was convinced God was not finished with me and the church. I then turned to each man with whom I had been entrusted to carry out this mission and asked if he would continue to lead with me. Two said yes. Two said they would serve out their terms as officers but could not say what they would do after that. One said he didn't think he could continue. We talked into the night, agreeing upon what needed to be done to address the needs of the congregation and what I would do to serve them and the church to meet those needs.

Within the next two weeks, two more families left the church. We told the other deacons of our conversations. Since that time, God has blessed our church. He had changed the leader's heart through testing; God could now transform the church. By the way, Ted was the chairman of deacons the next year! The other officer who took a wait-and-see position is a deacon officer again even now.

Why do I tell you this story? I tell it because it is the crucible in which I learned the heart of Jesus and the power of servant leadership. I began to understand what Jesus did when he washed the feet of his disciples. I learned that the power of leading as a servant comes from God's using a person who humbles himself (on his own or through the actions of others) to God's call on his life and who serves those who were entrusted to him in order to carry out that call. I learned that my greatest test of servant leadership may be to wash the feet of those who have the ability to ask for my resignation. That event has become a watershed in my relationship with God and with Christ's church.

This book grows out of my personal journey of learning to lead. The information on these pages comes from a personal crisis of choosing how I should lead among God's people. This book also grows out of the need to find and develop leaders who can carry out God's mission with me. This is not a complete picture of what I am learning, but it serves as a primer for those who want to learn to lead like Jesus.

Converse with the ideas on these pages. Let them challenge your presuppositions about leadership. Above all else, let them test your faith about who Jesus really is. That will make the difference not only in how you lead but in how you live your life.

JESUS' MODEL OF
SERVANT LEADERSHIP

WHAT did I learn when I laid aside every model of leadership I had read or heard about? Who was this Jesus I became reacquainted with when I took off my shoes and walked with him through the pages of the Bible? Let me tell you.

The essential lesson I learned from Jesus on leadership was that *he taught and embodied leadership as service.* Jesus was a Servant Leader in every sense of the concept. I would describe him as one who served his mission (in biblical language, "the will of [his] Father") and led by serving those he recruited to carry out that mission.

FOR JESUS, THE MISSION WAS TO BE THE MESSIAH. He was sent to bring salvation to the world as God's Sent One. He served that mission by living as the Suffering Servant Messiah. This mission was everything for Jesus. It was his purpose and direction for all he did while on earth—including his death.

....

> IF WE TAKE A HIGH-LEVEL LOOK AT JESUS'
> LIFE, WE SEE THAT EVERYTHING HE DID
> WAS IN SERVICE TO HIS MISSION.

....

FOR JESUS, THE MODEL OF LEADERSHIP WAS SERVANTHOOD. He was never self-serving. He led first as servant to his Father in heaven, who gave him his mission. If we take a high-level look at Jesus' life, we see that everything he did was in service to this mission. His personal mission was to serve not his own will but the will of his Father. He said, "For I have come down from heaven not to do my will but to do the will of him who sent me" (John 6:38).

THE MISSION—AND THE VISION

And what was the will of his Father? How did that translate into Jesus' life mission? At least three times Jesus provided what we would call a mission statement:

- ❖ When Jesus stood in his hometown synagogue, he read his mission statement from Isaiah: "The Spirit of the Lord is on me, because he has anointed me to preach good news to the poor. He has sent me to proclaim freedom for the prisoners and recovery of sight for the blind, to release the oppressed, to proclaim the year of the Lord's favor." *Isaiah 61:1-2; Luke 4:18-19*

- ❖ When Jesus stood among his disciples and defined greatness and being a leader in the kingdom of God, he couched his mission statement this way: "For even the Son of Man did not come to be served, but to serve, and to give his life as a ransom for many." *Mark 10:45*

- ❖ When Jesus stood in tax collector Zacchaeus's home, he stated it another way: "For the Son of Man came to seek and to save what was lost." *Luke 19:10*

Jesus articulated his mission in order to define what he was as Messiah. Where and how he led flowed from a clear sense of why he had come in the first place.

If Jesus was a servant to his mission, he led with a vision of what things would look like when he completed that mission. "What things would look like" was his vision of the Father's call on his life. Jesus cast a vision of how things would look for his followers—if they allowed him to be the Messiah God sent him to be. Jesus often described that vision of things to come as "The kingdom of God/heaven." Jesus painted word pictures in the form of stories to show people the vision of God for their lives. These stories, or parables, let people see the implications of Jesus' being the Sent One of God in their lives. Chapters 13 and 25 in Matthew's Gospel are collections of vision stories. Luke 15 is also filled with stories about why Jesus came and what lives looked like when God's love ruled in people's hearts. Jesus led others by casting a vision of how things would look when he completed his mission.

SEVEN PRINCIPLES TO LEAD AS JESUS LED

After seeking to understand the elements of Jesus' leadership style, I sought out timeless principles that described how Jesus led and that could be applied to my needs as a leader among God's people. Here are seven observations I discovered that describe how Jesus led as a servant.

1. Jesus humbled himself and allowed God to exalt him.
2. Jesus followed his Father's will rather than sought a position.
3. Jesus defined greatness as being a servant and being first as becoming a slave.

4. Jesus risked serving others because he trusted that he was God's Son.

5. Jesus left his place at the head table to serve the needs of others.

6. Jesus shared responsibility and authority with those he called to lead.

7. Jesus built a team to carry out a worldwide vision.

These seven observations about how Jesus led are the foundation for our seven principles of servant leadership. Each principle is based upon a teaching or an example of Jesus as he lived out his mission and led those he recruited to join him. Before you can lead as Jesus led, you and I must move beyond what I call a "head-table mentality."

HEAD-TABLE MENTALITY

One day, I found myself at a head table. My job was to introduce the speaker after the musician sang. As the speaker began his talk, everyone at the head table stood and moved to sit among those attending the conference. Everyone but me! The speaker, who picked up on those leaving the head table, said, "If you are at the head table and would like to move, you can at this time." Alone, I stood and said, "I'd love to!" We all laughed, and I walked red faced to sit at a table with those who served in the kitchen. From head table to kitchen-worker status—in front of my peer group! What a demotion!

As the blood returned to the rest of my body, Jesus' story about where to sit at big meals came to mind. He taught:

> When someone invites you to a wedding feast [or conference], do not take the place of honor [at the head table], for a person more distinguished than you may have been invited. If so, the

host who invited both of you will come and say to you, "Give this man your seat." Then, humiliated, you will have to take the least important place. But when you are invited, take the lowest place, so that when your host comes, he will say to you, "Friend, move up to a better place." Then you will be honored in the presence of all your fellow guests. For everyone who exalts himself will be humbled, and he who humbles himself will be exalted. LUKE 14:8-11

As I reflected on my social blunder and the speaker's words about leadership, I realized that I had done what was typical of many who sit at head tables. When given a position, we happily accept the status that goes with it and somehow believe we no longer need to go near the kitchen. I was suffering from head-table mentality. I had accepted the myth that those who sit at the head table are somehow more important than those who serve in the kitchen. I even had perpetuated that myth by nonverbally resisting a place among the servers. I wondered if the people in my church suffered from this mentality.

....

WE WHO LEAD OFTEN OVERLOOK THAT
THE TRUE PLACE OF CHRISTLIKE
LEADERSHIP IS OUT IN THE CROWD
RATHER THAN UP AT THE HEAD TABLE.

....

I realized that we who lead often overlook the fact that the true place of Christlike leadership is out in the crowd rather than up at the head table. People who follow Christ's model of leadership would never be embarrassed to find themselves among the kitchen help. Such a leader is comfortable working with those who serve in the background and gladly works alongside them until they complete the job. Head tables are optional for leaders who follow Jesus. Service, not status, is the goal of this kind of leader.

BRING BACK THE TOWEL AND WASHBASIN

Too many organizations, homes, businesses, and schools struggle because they lack men and women who lead as Jesus did. Head tables have replaced the towel and washbasin as symbols of leadership among God's people. Often those recognized as leaders in the church, for example, hold positions elected by friends and family. Some of these leaders love sitting at head tables but never go near the kitchen (or nursery). Leaders in civic groups may seek to push their personal agendas rather than work with those in their care to meet the goals of the group.

Churches, organizations, and the communities they serve, however, need leaders who know how God has made and gifted them for service and who willingly serve Christ and those placed in their care. These groups need leaders who have skills to equip others and to "team with them" in ministry. We need leaders who will step down from the head table and serve in the kitchen. Ministries and organizations will survive in the twenty-first century when men and women stop following self-conceived concepts of leadership and adopt Jesus' teachings and examples.

....

HEAD TABLES HAVE REPLACED THE TOWEL
AND WASHBASIN AS SYMBOLS OF
LEADERSHIP AMONG GOD'S PEOPLE.

....

Service-centered leadership has found its way into current discussions about leadership. The writings of businesspeople like

Robert Greenleaf, Peter Block, Stephen Covey, and Max DePree have called leaders to a service-oriented model of leadership. In the marketplace, the pendulum has swung from personality-centered leadership to character-based leadership. I believe interest in principles of servant leadership has grown out of a desire for organizations to be led by those who will serve not themselves but those they lead. Our culture has wearied of the leadership models of Attila the Hun and rogue warriors. We are seeking leaders who consider us more than a means to an end.

The time is ripe to bring Jesus' principles of leadership into the discussion of leadership. This should happen in the church especially, because leaders in the church—who should have been paving the way to service-oriented leadership—have actually gravitated toward the self-serving forms of leadership that are now being discarded by secular thinking.

HOW DO WE
LEAD BY SERVING?

SERVANT and leader stand together as a model for those
entrusted with the well-being of a group. Leaders who follow
the example and teachings of Jesus will lead first as servants.
If that is the case, how does a leader serve and still lead?

I realize that for people today who are well versed in
leadership studies, the concept of servant leader causes a
significant mental block. I once addressed a group of innovative church leaders. As I described the seven principles of servant leadership, I could see from their faces that they were
comparing the principles against concepts of leadership they
had learned from conventional wisdom. I struggled to
explain how a servant could lead and how leaders could still
lead while serving others. At the end of the session, I knew
that I had not completed the connection between leadership
and service.

The link between the two concepts came to me two weeks
later when a friend asked me, "What is your passion?" The
answer to that question helped me realize that my passion was

the mission! Mission (and the vision of that mission) was the connection between service and leadership. I rushed back to Jesus' model of servant leadership and saw how his mission connected his service and leadership. I found that I could lead through both conflict and synergy because I had become servant to God's mission to make disciples in my life and through the church. My leadership style had become that of servant to those on mission with me so we could carry out God's mission in our lives as a unified body of believers. In the short weeks that followed, I was able to move from a description of servant leadership to a working definition:

> A servant leader—
> *serves the mission* and
> *leads by serving* those on mission with him.

The mission is everything.

Mission is everything for the servant leader. The mission that God or someone in authority entrusts to the leader is the focus of every decision and action. True servant leadership begins when the leader humbles himself to carry out the mission entrusted to him rather than his personal agenda.

This service to the mission creates the passion that is essential for a leader's effectiveness. Lyle Schaller told a group of church leaders, "I think passion is the critical variable. It has taken me a long time to come around to that, but if a pastor does not have a passion for the mission, you can forget the rest. I would insist the number one quality of a leader be passion."[1] Bill Easum concurred with Schaller when he said, "It all goes back to why we are doing this. . . . It's the mission . . . and the pastor and key leaders simply must have a passion for the mission. It is more than just maintaining or even growing a church, but believing your church can reach an entire city or a region; believing they can make a difference."[2] Servant leaders have passion for the mission because the mission is so paramount in their lives that they have literally become servants to it. This passion for the mission drives the leader to recruit and empower others to join him on that mission.

A servant leader is also servant to those on mission with him. While serving the mission, servant leaders actively recruit and build up others to join them. The leader becomes servant to those who have joined him when he provides adequate vision, direction, correction, and resources to carry out the mission entrusted to the group. The leader serves when he equips others and "teams" with them to reach the goal of mission together.

....

LEADERSHIP BEGINS WHEN A GOD-REVEALED MISSION CAPTURES A PERSON.

....

Leadership begins when a God-revealed mission captures a person. This person turns leader as he becomes servant to the mission. Before mission, there is no need or motivation to lead. The leader then sees a picture of what the mission looks like in the future and casts his vision of that mission to others. Vision is a leader's unique rendering of the mission. Leadership turns to service when the leader equips those recruited to carry out the now-shared mission. Leadership is complete when the equipper empowers those he has equipped into teams to maximize resources in order to execute the mission. Simply put: Servant leadership is passionate service to the mission and to those who join the leader on that mission.

FOUR KEY CONCEPTS

The four operative concepts of servant leadership are: Mission, Vision, Equip, and Team. *Mission* is God's call on your life. You know what your mission is when you can complete the statement, "God called me to _____."
Vision is your unique take on that mission. You can state your vision by completing the statement, "When the mission is complete it will look like this: _____."
Equip is how you train others to join you on mission to complete the vision. *Team* is how you mobilize those you have equipped to carry out the mission beyond your departure.

If you look at the model below, you will see that *mission* and *vision* are above the horizontal line. When a person becomes servant to the mission and vision, he also becomes a leader. This corresponds with Jesus' mission as Messiah and vision of the kingdom of God.

	MESSIAH (mission)	KINGDOM (vision)
THE SERVANT	Servant	Leads
LEADERSHIP MODEL	Leader	Serves
OF JESUS	FOLLOW ME (equip)	THE 12 (team)

Below the horizontal line are the elements of *equip* and *team*. When a servant to the mission recruits a group of people to carry out that mission with him, he becomes a leader who serves. He serves by equipping those on mission with him and mobilizing them into teams to reach the vision cast for them. These elements correspond to Jesus' serving his disciples by calling them to follow him and by building the Twelve into a ministry team.

This model is not just for people in assigned or elected leadership positions in a church or corporation. A mother can be a servant leader. Kim, my wife and the mother of our two daughters, has become a servant to God's mission in her life. That mission as a mother is to raise godly children. Living out that mission has meant setting aside her personal desires for career and sometimes even friendships. Her vision of God's call on her life as a mother is that she will teach our daughters to be witnesses or ministers of God's love wherever they find themselves: at home, with friends, at school, at church, or on their competitive teams. Kim leads our daughters by equipping them to be witnesses and ministers and serves them as she provides direction, correction, and resources to carry out God's mission in their lives. She is seeking to build them into a team of two who will carry out the mission after she is no longer around them. The servant leadership model applies at home, in church, and in the marketplace.

Heart makes it happen.

A servant's heart is essential for this kind of leadership. This state of heart allows God to reveal and define the life-driving mission in a person's life. This condition also brings the leader into the lives of those she leads. Without that spirit, the leader remains aloof and distant from those carrying out the mission with her. A servant's heart allows the leader to put aside her own agenda in order to carry out that mission. I am convinced that only a relationship with the Servant Leader, Jesus Christ, can produce such a heart condition.

WHY DO WE LEAD DIFFERENTLY FROM JESUS?

Jesus' priorities in leadership are different from how we tend to lead today. This is because our priorities come from our natural tendencies rather than our spiritual resources. J. Oswald Sanders, author of *Spiritual Leadership*,[3] has rightly compared natural and spiritual leadership tendencies:

Natural	Spiritual
Self-confident	Confident in God
Knows men	Knows God
Makes own decisions	Seeks to find God's will
Ambitious	Self-effacing
Originates own methods	Finds and follows God's methods
Enjoys commanding others	Delights to obey God
Motivated by personal considerations	Motivated by love for God and man
Independent	God-dependent

The differences between those who lead out of their natural motives and those who lead from a spiritual base are clear. Jesus modeled the power of authentic, spiritual leadership.

How can everyday men and women adopt the leadership of Jesus? He was, after all, God! How do those of us who know our true selves lead as Jesus did? We can lead Jesus' way only when we obey his teachings and examples. It begins by becoming servant to the Servant Leader. That relationship will yield both mission and vision for our lives.

THE S WORD

Submission to God and to the divine mission for your life is the first step to servant leadership. You will never become a servant leader until you first become servant *to* the Leader. Your mission and purpose in life spring from the relationship you have with God. While many people invite you to determine your own destiny, God calls you to live out a divine plan through your life. Knowing and living that life mission begin in a personal relationship with God through Jesus Christ.

....
YOU WILL NEVER BECOME A SERVANT LEADER UNTIL YOU FIRST BECOME SERVANT TO THE LEADER.
....

The issue of submission to Jesus as Master is central to our discussion. You and I do not naturally submit to anyone or anything. Insist that I be your slave, and you have a civil-rights case on your hands! American history illustrates what happens when one human enslaves another. We resist submission to another person with every fiber of our cholesterol-free lifestyles. In a culture where the individual has reached godlike status, submitting to anyone or anything outside ourselves is beyond reason. Self-interest soars high above service in our hierarchy of interests. These attitudes are part of our cultural thinking. They are also the very feelings that prevent us from knowing the freedom that comes from giving ourselves to Christ.

Jesus said, "If anyone would come after me, he must deny himself and take up his cross and follow me" (Matt. 16:24). Denying—not embracing—self is the first step to becoming a servant leader. We will cover this fact more fully in our discussion of the first principle of servant leadership in the next chapter.

If you desire to lead as Jesus led, you must desire first to follow Jesus; this is how leadership training among God's people begins.

A LOOK AHEAD

Each chapter of this book will focus on one of Jesus' principles of leadership. These principles will serve as guidelines for developing a personal model of servant leadership in whatever context God has placed you. I suggest that you take off your shoes, put on the sandals of a disciple, and follow Jesus through the pages of the Gospels. By following Jesus, you will see how Jesus wants us to lead among his people.

Let me remind you that this book is secondary to the good news of Jesus Christ. My prayer is that reading this book will lead you to read the Bible—again or for the first time. I want you to see that following Jesus has practical implications for how you live your life, not just more information from which to form an opinion. I want you to know the power of being a servant leader like Jesus. My desire is for you to know more about yourself and God's plan for your life after walking through these pages. Don't look for human insights. Look for the purposes of God for your life.

You can read this book as a study guide to the leadership style of Jesus. You will find contemporary applications and references to works on leadership and how they pertain to a servant model of leadership. I will introduce you to familiar and not-so-well-known writers on leadership. If you are a leader, this book will give you insights into how you can become more effective as a leader. If you don't consider yourself a leader, this material will help you understand how leaders lead and how you can be a better follower. This book can serve as a manual for leadership in the home, church, or marketplace.

You can use this material as a devotional guide to discover the love of God as revealed in God's Son/Servant, Jesus. Following Jesus is ultimately about knowing God. If you walk away from this book and only know more about God, I have not accomplished my goal for this book. My prayer is that you will encounter the God of all ages by seeking the One sent to bring you salvation and an eternal relationship with the God who created you. My hope is that if you do not know God as revealed in the person of Jesus, you will meet him in these pages.

The principles in this book build upon one another somewhat because they tend to follow Jesus' teachings and examples of leadership chronologically. They also reflect a deepening relationship between Jesus and his followers. You, however, can study each principle independently of the others. Each principle stands alone as part of the entire servant-leadership model.

Here's a look at what you will be reading:

Principle #1: Humble your heart

"Servant leaders humble themselves and wait for God to exalt them" (based on Luke 14:7-11). This principle comes from Jesus' story about choosing places of honor at a banquet. Servant leaders humble themselves to the mission entrusted to them. They also wait expectantly for God to exalt them—in God's timing. Servant leaders trust that the Host will choose those he wants at the head table of leadership.

Principle #2: First be a follower

"Servant leaders follow Jesus rather than seek a position" (based on Mark 10:32-40). This tenet comes from James and John's request of Jesus that they sit on his right and left when he came into his glory. I will describe this biblical event and draw applications from our natural tendency to equate leadership with position. Jesus, on the other hand, taught that suffering for him comes before reigning with him.

Principle #3: Find greatness in service

"Servant leaders give up personal rights to find greatness in service to others" (based on Mark 10:45). The other ten disciples did not appreciate James and John's boldness with Jesus. When the Master saw that they had become indignant with their peers, he defined greatness and being first among the followers of Christ. Greatness begins with those who become servants to the mission of the group and those teamed with them to carry out that mission. The best example of this principle is Jesus' own life.

Principle #4: Take risks

"Servant leaders can risk serving others because they trust that God is in control of their lives" (based on John 13:3). Only when you trust God with absolute control of your life can you risk losing yourself in service to others. Trusting God includes believing that God is working with at least five "raw materials" to form you into a unique servant leader. Those raw materials are your spiritual gifts, experiences, relational style, vocational skills, and enthusiasm. These elements make up your S.E.R.V.E. profile.

Principle #5: Take up the towel

"Servant leaders take up Jesus' towel of servanthood to meet the needs of others" (based on John 13:4-11). Jesus stepped down from his place at the Passover meal to set an example for his disciples. He took up the towel and washbasin of a slave to model his mission and show his love for those he recruited to carry out that mission after his ascension. We will discover the power of servant leadership as modeled by the Suffering Servant of God.

Principle #6: Share responsibility and authority

"Servant leaders share their responsibility and authority with others to meet a greater need" (based on Acts 6:1-6). Jesus equipped his disciples to carry out a worldwide vision. He shared both responsibility and authority with them to make disciples of all people. Those same disciples shared their responsibility and authority with their peers in order to meet a need greater than their resources could handle alone. We will review five steps to EQUIP someone. Servant leaders encourage others to serve, qualify others for service, understand the needs of those they equip, instruct others in their specific tasks, and pray for those they invite into ministry.

Principle #7: Build a team

"Servant leaders multiply their leadership by empowering others to lead" (based on Mark 6:7). Leadership of a team is the highest expression of servant leadership. This is true because team leadership embodies each of the principles of servant leadership. Servant leaders serve best when they team with others to accomplish the mission. We will review four steps to building a ministry team.

Throughout the discussion of the seven principles, I will make application of Jesus' model of leadership into marriage, parenthood, and the marketplace. I believe you will find these applications surprising to the extent that you will discover you really are a leader if you are living out God's call on your life.

The world wants to know what a servant leader after the model and teaching of Jesus looks like. People want to see how Jesus' model of service to God and others lives out in a person's life at the beginning of a new millennium.

LEADERSHIP IS NOT SOMETHING YOU PURSUE. LEADERSHIP IS SOMETHING OTHERS GIVE TO YOU

No matter how smart, talented, and persuasive you are naturally or by training, you are not the leader until the group you are leading says so. The mantle of leadership is bestowed on you by those who grasp your mission and choose to follow you. You cannot wrest that mantle from those who do not share your mission or who refuse to follow you. You earn the place of leader through authentic relationships and character. Whether you hold a position of leadership or not, to lead, you must gain the trust of those you have recruited or who have been entrusted to you. The follower holds the final power to determine the leader.

YOU ARE NOT THE LEADER UNTIL THE GROUP YOU ARE LEADING SAYS SO.

I have learned this truth as a husband, a father, and a pastor. A husband cannot lead his wife until he first serves her through acts of love and kindness. A father will never be the leader of a family unless his children acknowledge his place of authority over them. How do they learn that? Children learn that a father is a leader through his loving service to them through training and discipline. A pastor may be given the title and biblical position of leader, but he will never lead a group of people until that group gives him the freedom and trust to lead them. *How does any assigned leader actually become the accepted leader of the group?* The answer to that question is found in this book. If you will apply these seven principles of servant leadership as taught and modeled by Jesus, I am convinced you will become more effective as a leader, and those who have been entrusted to you will be more likely to place on you the mantle of leadership.

EVERY GREAT LEADER IS A SERVANT LEADER

A great leader is great because he lives—without compromise—the call to mission on his life. He is also great because he inspires others to carry out that mission with him. I believe Jesus was (and is) a great servant leader because he served his Father's mission without compromise and has inspired many people over many centuries to carry it out. I can also say that I believe Jesus was the greatest leader because his mission was for all people for all time. Even great leaders in history only affect their space on the timeline and beyond. Jesus affected all creation for all time. His life, death, and resurrection served the greatest need of people for all time: to have a personal relationship with the God who created us.

FOR STUDY AND REFLECTION

- When you read the term *servant leadership* for the first time, what did you think/feel?

- Read through the seven statements describing how Jesus led. Put a check mark by the ones that are new to you or that you may have questions about.

- What leadership issues are you facing in your life at this time? You may be a parent, CEO, manager, or church leader. Make a list of those issues you hope this book will address.

- Have you ever thought of Jesus as a leader? If so, what characteristics describe him best for you? Have you ever viewed Jesus as a servant? If so, how? If not, why not?

- Can you articulate the four elements of servant leadership for your life? What is God's mission for your life? Can you paint a picture of what your life will look like when that mission is complete? How are you leading by equipping those who are on mission with you? Write the names of those you are building into a ministry team.

- Would you describe yourself as one who has submitted your life to Jesus and as one who is actively seeking to model your leadership style after him? If not, how would you describe your relationship to Jesus at this time?

Endnotes

1. Quoted by Carol Childress in *NetFax,* a publication of Leadership Network (Number 84, 10 November 1997). For information about this service, contact Leadership Network at 1-800-765-5323 or www.leadnet.org, which contains this and back issues of *NetFax.*

2. Ibid.

3. J. Oswald Sanders, *Spiritual Leadership* (Chicago: Moody Press, 1967), 38.

HUMBLE YOUR HEART

TRUE greatness, true leadership, is achieved
not by reducing men to one's service but in
giving oneself in selfless service to them.
J. OSWALD SANDERS *Spiritual Leadership*

IF YOU truly want to be great, then the direction you
must go is down. You must descend into greatness.
BILL HYBELS *Descending into Greatness*

TRUE leaders are, by definition, both
magnanimous and humble.
WARREN BENNIS *Why Leaders Can't Lead*

WHOEVER humbles himself like this child
is the greatest in the kingdom of heaven.
JESUS *Matthew 18:4*

MORE than any other single way, the grace
of humility is worked into our lives
through the Discipline of service.
RICHARD J. FOSTER *Celebration of Discipline*

SOMETIMES I like to imagine what certain events in the Bible were like—how they felt and looked and sounded. Remember the scene in Luke 14?

Jesus' disciples are standing along a wall in the courtyard. They appear to be an island of outcasts in the middle of an upper-class sea. A Pharisee has invited Jesus over to meet some of his religious buddies. Having the newest popular evangelist over to your house is a favorite sport among religious leaders. A banquet table is set. Jesus talks with the host and some of his synagogue buddies.

Someone announces that the meal is ready, and like horses in a chariot race, people make their way to seats around the tables. Some push their way to the head table.

Jesus observes this mad rush to the front. He turns to his followers and says, "When someone invites you to a banquet, do not grab a place of honor. Someone more important than you may have been invited. If that is so, the host who invited both of you will come up to you and say, 'Give my friend your seat.' Then humiliated, you will have to take a less important place.

"So, when you are invited to a banquet, take the least important place, so that when your host comes he will say to you, 'Friend, what are you doing back here? Move up to a better place by me!' Then you will be honored in front of all the other guests. Here's the punch line: everyone who exalts himself will be humbled, and everyone who humbles himself will be exalted."

After speaking, Jesus quietly reclines on a couch away from the host. His disciples continue to linger against the wall.

Thus, we have been given the first principle of servant leadership:

Servant leaders humble themselves and wait for God to exalt them.

HUMILITY
THE LIVING EXAMPLE

JESUS' teaching challenged a common assumption in his day. Pushing and shoving to get to the head table was natural. It was how young Pharisees got ahead. Who would argue? Sitting up front meant one had arrived at the top.

Jesus' object lesson at the Pharisee's home came to my mind as I sat among the kitchen workers at the event I told you about earlier. The rush to the best places is as real today as it was in Jesus' time. Religious leaders still seek places of prominence among their peers. Even in some large churches and religious organizations people seeking control pursue real estate and positions of power. Leaders in all sectors of business and education still seek leadership and push to the front to gain those places. According to our success-oriented society, bigger is better and closer to the top means, well, closer to the top.

Getting to the head table is a natural priority in a culture of achievement. Head tables have become a finish line in the great rat race. Who would argue with someone wanting to sit closest to a friend in high places? Who would criticize a little aggressive effort in order to succeed?

Several years ago, I walked into the office of a Christian businessman. On his desk was the sign "If the meek inherit the earth, what do us tigers get?" The world's thinking had changed his understanding of the gospel. For him, *meek* meant weak, and tigers—not the slow and soft—topped the food chain. This man's attitude was similar to that of many contemporary Christians. We wonder, *What's the big deal about the head of the table? Why did Jesus say what he did to the people at this dinner? And would he still want to address that topic—in our lives?*

....

JESUS TAUGHT THAT HEAD-TABLE SEATS ARE "BY INVITATION ONLY" RATHER THAN "BY HOOK OR BY CROOK."

....

Jesus' direct challenge to our natural desire to get ahead is what makes his story so biting. Jesus saw something we overlook: As long as leaders worry about who sits at the head table, they have little time for the people they are called to serve. We don't see opportunities for service while our eyes are fixed on the competition. Jesus taught that head table seats are "by invitation only" rather than "by hook or crook."

The first time I presented this topic to a group of more than one hundred people, I was nervous. When I quoted Jesus, I said, "He who exalts himself will be humbled, and he who humbles himself will be exhausted." We all laughed, but then we agreed that this was how most of us felt about humbling ourselves! We feared that if we humbled ourselves, we would exhaust ourselves trying to do everything people asked us to do! We feared becoming doormats for others to walk on.

But actually the opposite is true. Jesus says that if we will humble ourselves and learn from him, he will give us rest (Matt. 11:28). True humility does not lead to exhaustion but frees us to serve others. In God's kingdom, achievement is not the goal, but we will never grasp that until we've learned humility. Then we can relax and serve, knowing that any honor that comes to us is given, not earned.

ARE WE WILLING TO FACE SOME FACTS?

Jesus' comments point out some facts about life.

"A person more distinguished than you may have been invited." *Luke 14:8*

Wherever we go, someone is "more distinguished" than we are. We are not as important as we would like to think. Someone will always outrank me or you. Isn't it better for us to realize and accept this than to be fighting for prestige we don't have? No one wants to be asked to sit somewhere else.

If you assume more honor than you have, you will end up embarrassed in front of your peers. *Luke 14:9*

So you've pushed your way to the front, and you've just settled in to enjoy conversation with the prestigious people, and someone nudges you. You feel your face get hot when—oh no—the host himself asks you as politely as he can, "Could you move to that table over there? We already have a guest for this place—see the name card?" On the other hand, it's so gratifying when the host comes to get you, saying, "Hey—we've saved a place up front for you!" A humble spirit can lead to being honored by others. When you take that backseat, you're actually trusting God instead of your own efforts to push your way through. And true humility eliminates the burning need to be honored in the first place.

Final recognition comes from God.
The world says, "Work your way to the head table." Jesus says, "Take a seat in the back. I'll choose who sits up front." How do you get ahead if you are waiting on God rather than making things happen yourself?

Getting ahead was never part of the deal with Jesus. The goal of a disciple is to please the Teacher, not climb to the top of the heap. Those who follow Jesus willingly humble themselves because their Teacher was humble. Jesus seldom described himself personally. On one occasion, however, he described himself as "gentle and humble in heart" (Matt. 11:29). Jesus also said, "Therefore, whoever humbles himself like this child is the greatest in the kingdom of heaven" (Matt. 18:4). Childlike humility is a requirement for service among God's people. Competitive ambition does not fit the profile of a person who follows Jesus.

DOWNWARD ON A PATH TO GREATNESS

Jesus lived the humility he taught. When the apostle Paul urged the Christians in Philippi to serve each other, he recalled Jesus' life and reminded his friends of their true source of strength. He told them, "In humility consider others better than yourselves. Each of you should look not only to your own interests, but also to the interests of others" (Phil. 2:3-4). *How do you do that?* the readers must have asked themselves. Paul answered when he wrote, "Your attitude should be the same as that of Christ Jesus" (Phil. 2:5).

Paul then described Jesus' humble service of taking on the form of a servant and dying on the cross for others. Paul said to be like Jesus, who "made himself nothing, taking the very nature of a servant, being made in human likeness. And being found in appearance as a man, he humbled himself and became obedient to death—even death on a cross!" (Phil. 2:7-8).

The key phrase in this passage is "he humbled himself" (Phil. 2:8). *Humble* is the same word Jesus used in his story to the disciples about seeking out places at the head table. Jesus taught humility because it was at the core of who he was. It enabled him to follow God's plan for his life. The person who leads as Jesus leads will take his approach. From the very beginning, Jesus was out not to honor himself but to follow God's will.

Bill Hybels says this may be "the most countercultural chapter in the Bible."[1] Jesus left the perfect setup in heaven to take on the form of a human and lose his life for others. This downward mobility is against the flow of cultural values. Hybels states the truth of the passage:

> The message of Philippians is this: If you want to be truly great, then the direction you must go is down. You must descend into greatness. At the heart of this paradox is still another paradox: Greatness is not a measure of self-will, but rather self-abandonment. The more you lose, the more you gain.[2]

Jesus "did not consider equality with God something to be grasped, but made himself nothing" (Phil. 2:6-7). He took on the form of a servant, and he humbled himself to the will of his Father. Jesus' story has a "riches to rags"[3] beginning. His life was a picture of humble service. Anyone who follows him will find herself on a downward path to greatness.

Jesus never sought earthly recognition. He came to carry out the mission his Father had given him. Humble service to his Father defined the life of Jesus. Those who model their lives after Jesus will have the same said of them.

Henri Nouwen drew this conclusion about Christian leadership modeled after Jesus:

The way of the Christian leader is not the way of upward mobility in which our world has invested so much, but the way of downward mobility ending on the cross. This might sound morbid and masochistic, but for those who have heard the voice of the first love and said "yes" to it, the downward-moving way of Jesus is the way to the joy and the peace of God, a joy and peace that is not of this world.

Here we touch the most important quality of Christian leadership in the future. It is not a leadership of power and control, but leadership of powerlessness and humility in which the suffering servant of God, Jesus Christ, is made manifest.[4]

The key phrase in Philippians 2 is "God exalted him" (v. 9). *Exalt* is the same word Jesus used in his illustration at the banquet. God exalted his Son after Jesus humbled himself in obedience to death on the cross. Peter, who was present at Jesus' lesson on humility recorded in Luke 14, told the first Christians to "humble yourselves, therefore, under God's mighty hand, that he may lift you up in due time" (1 Pet. 5:6). *Exalt* in the dictionary of faith means God lifts up those who have humbled themselves before him and his purposes.

Are you a leader after the example of Jesus? If so, make a practice of humbling yourself, taking the lesser position, looking for ways to be attentive to other people. Exaltation is God's choice, not yours. Christian leaders—most of all—should be known for acting counter to the culture of success. God will choose those who will be up front.

Humble and wait are not in every list of leadership traits. Humility, like meekness, can be perceived as weakness. "Never let them see you sweat" is more than a deodorant slogan. Those who pass on the freeway shoulder shout, "Waiting is for losers!" Waiting on God sounds too slow and too spiritual for ambitious souls. Earthly perception and divine reality, however, rarely match. Two distinguishing character qualities of a servant leader are humility and the ability to wait.

....

TWO DISTINGUISHING CHARACTER
QUALITIES OF A SERVANT LEADER ARE
HUMILITY AND THE ABILITY TO WAIT.

....

The Bible places great value on humility. It teaches that "humility comes before honor" (Prov. 15:33). James, an apostle who followed Jesus, wrote: "Humble yourselves before the Lord, and he will lift you up" (James 4:10). Scripture described Moses as "a very humble man, *more humble than anyone else on the face of the earth*" (Num. 12:3, italics mine). The Bible described Moses this way when Miriam and Aaron challenged the law-giver's leadership. Although the leader had every right to let God wreak havoc in their lives because of their attempted coup, Moses intervened with God on their behalf. Only a humble man can represent the interests of people who are critical of him.

Humility begins when you have a true picture of yourself before God and God's call on your life.

We perceive that we are important when we compare ourselves to others, and Jesus warned against that. Jesus said, "Do not judge, or you too will be judged" (Matt. 7:1). This teaching does not mean we are to deny absolute truths in order to tolerate the sins of others. Jesus was saying that we are not to compare ourselves with others so that we'll feel better about ourselves. We don't get our worth by looking at other people; God has already declared our worth through the gift of salvation.

Biblical humility requires that we stop the comparison game. If we can't gauge our progress by looking at others, how will we assess ourselves? By holding our lives up against God's call to us. By comparing our character to the character of Jesus. No other standards apply. And when we use the Lord of the universe as our standard, it's much easier to be humble!

Humility is also a by-product of seeing yourself in relation to the task you have been entrusted with as the leader. Peter Drucker writes that a basic competence to lead "regardless of the weather" requires the willingness to realize how unimportant you are compared to the task. Leaders need objectivity, a certain detachment. They subordinate themselves to the task but don't identify themselves *with* the task. The task remains bigger than they are and also separate from them. The worst thing you can say about a leader is that on the day he left, the organization collapsed. When that happens, it means the so-called leader had sucked the place dry. He hasn't built something that would last with or without him. He may have been an effective operator, but he has not created a vision.[5]

You can assign yourself to a lower position when you realize that you are a servant to the mission or goal God has given you. Max DePree notes that self-assurance plus humility gives confidence to those who follow the leader. He writes, "A combination of self-confidence and humility seems to me to be crucial, for this oxymoronic quality makes it possible for the group to be decisive."[6] Warren Bennis lists humility among the "basic ingredients of leadership."[7] Humility produced by the presence of God brings a Christ-centered confidence in the leader.

Go back to Drucker's statement about the willingness to realize how unimportant you are compared to the task. That is the beginning of real humility. Say, for example, you have been asked to be the block chairperson for your local American Heart

Association membership drive. Your responsibility may seem manageable, and you could become proud of your contribution to raise money to fund research and care for those with heart disease. Until you realize the size of the ultimate task: to raise money for an entire nation of millions who suffer from heart disease. It is hard to be self-centered when you realize the full extent of what you and all the other block chairpersons are trying to do! Humility comes when you see yourself in light of the task you have been given.

Humility allows God to work in a person's life.
Without humility, God can have no place in a person's life because ego has become god. When the ego is in control, how can God have influence in one's day-to-day decisions? We all admire a leader who has confidence. In fact, in this achieving culture, the ones with a lot of self-confidence usually become leaders! But are they leaders in God's sense of the term?

....

THE DIFFERENCE BETWEEN PRIDE AND AUTHENTIC CONFIDENCE IS THE SOURCE.

....

The difference between pride and authentic confidence is the source. God grants confidence to those who trust him. Divinely directed confidence is the certainty that God has created you, bought you through the death of his Son, and called you out to join in the worldwide mission of hope.

Ego, on the other hand, produces pride. Anthony DeMello puts it this way:

> Disciple: I have come to offer you my service.
> Master: If you dropped the "I," service would automatically follow.

> You could give all your goods to feed the poor and your
> body to be burnt and yet not have love at all.
> Keep your goods and abandon the "I." Don't burn
> the body: burn the ego. Love will automatically follow.[8]

Pride is the opposite of humility and God-centered confidence. Pride is an inflated view of who we really are. It is arrogant self-worship.[9] It is *God* spelled *E-G-O*. Ken Blanchard, coauthor of *The One Minute Manager* (New York: Berkley Books, 1981), reminds us that ego stands for "edging God out."[10] He goes on to say, "When we start to get a distorted image of our own importance and see ourselves as the center of the universe, we lose touch with who we really are as children of God."[11] This "distorted image of our own importance" keeps us out of the lives of others and focused on what we alone want and think we need.

As a pastor, I have the hard job of working with people whose marriages are falling apart. No divorce comes in an instant. It takes two people and sometimes years of events for a marriage relationship to fall apart. When I finally get to meet with the couple, things are usually pretty bad. I have observed over the years that more times than not, one of the partners has developed a self-protective attitude. The entire conversation is about him and what he deserves and what she has not done for him and how she . . . and so on. I am not a trained counselor, but I can tell the difference between someone who is protecting himself and someone who is willing to reconcile the situation. That difference revolves around the person's ego. God cannot work in that relationship until both people are willing to take the "I" out of the conversation and serve the needs of their partner. God will not work until both lay down their egos and humbly care for the other. Ego blocks God's work. Humility opens the door for reconciliation.

LEARNING TO BE HUMBLE;
LEARNING TO WAIT

DO YOU feel that God is calling you to be a leader? If so, you must let go of pride. Pride ruins leaders. It will push you to seek places you think you deserve rather than where God has chosen you to serve. Pride sets you above others and insists that you deserve service from *them*. Pride blinds you to your weaknesses and to others' strengths. Pride drives you to build barriers rather than bridges. And pride will always place itself ahead of the mission and ahead of the people who are involved with you to carry out the mission.

The Bible contains many warnings against pride. For example:

❖ The Lord detests all the proud of heart.

❖ Pride goes before destruction, a haughty spirit before a fall.

❖ Better to be lowly in spirit and among the oppressed than to share plunder with the proud.[12]

....

PRIDE WILL PUSH YOU TO SEEK PLACES YOU THINK YOU DESERVE RATHER THAN WHERE GOD HAS CHOSEN YOU TO SERVE.

....

Jesus began his design for discipleship with this statement: "Blessed are the poor in spirit, for theirs is the kingdom of heaven" (Matt. 5:3). Poverty of spirit signaled readiness for the kingdom. Jesus told stories about humble widows and repentant tax collectors whom God honored because of their humility.

But isn't some pride necessary to carry out the vision God has given you? You have to be confident if you're going to accomplish God's plans, don't you? The issue is not merely pride but character as well. By itself, your pride will produce arrogance. But if the pride you experience is built on the character that God is developing in you, it will produce a quiet confidence. This is the type of confidence that can see a vision through to its fulfillment. It is a confidence not dependent upon our own abilities and drive but upon God's ability to bless the world through us.

An arrogant young visionary

Joseph was his father's favorite son, and he wore a richly ornamented coat to prove it. God came to Joseph when he was seventeen and gave him a vision for the future. Someday, according to the dreams, Joseph's eleven brothers would bow down to him. Joseph was "well-built and handsome" (Gen. 39:6). Joseph had everything a person needs to become a leader: a parent's blessing at age seventeen, a vision for the future, and recognized physical gifts.

All of those things, however, resulted in arrogance in Joseph's life. His brothers hated him, and they plotted to kill him. Only after his big brother intervened did they decide to sell him as a slave instead.

What did these events have to do with Joseph's living out

God's plan for his life? The cistern and slavery were tools God used to turn Joseph's arrogance into godly confidence. God molded Joseph's character through these events.

Character is the balance to giftedness. Joseph's life got harder before it got easier. It was not until Joseph's pride was based upon the work of God rather than his personal abilities and dreams that God elevated him to a place where he could see those dreams fulfilled.

....

CHARACTER IS THE BALANCE TO GIFTEDNESS.

....

Paul and James on pride

Paul, the apostle, knew about the importance of character. He knew about Joseph, too. In his letter to the Christians in Rome, he reminded them that "suffering produces perseverance; perseverance, character; and character, hope. And hope does not disappoint" (Rom. 5:3-5). James echoed Paul's words when he wrote, "Consider it pure joy, my brothers, whenever you face trials . . . because you know that the testing of your faith develops perseverance" (James 1:2-3). Trials are the crucible in which our character is purified. It is this character that results in godly confidence and thus equips us to live out God's visions. Leaders who live God's dream are not always the most flamboyant, popular, and gifted people. They are the people who have been humble enough to be shaped by God, who have developed the character to act on God's behalf.

Humility and service

How do we learn humility? How is this character trait formed in our hearts? We learn humility the same way we learn every other aspect of the Christian life: by following Jesus. Brennan Manning writes:

> We learn humility directly from the Lord Jesus in whatever way he wishes to teach us. Most often we learn humility through humiliations. What is humility? It is the stark realization and acceptance of the fact that I am totally dependent upon God's love and mercy. It grows through a stripping away of all self-sufficiency. Humility is not caught by repeating pious phrases. It is accomplished by the hand of God. It is Job on the dung hill all over again as God reminds us that he is our only true hope.[13]

Those who follow Jesus find themselves treated like Jesus. Out of those experiences they begin to understand the difference between self-centered pride and humble confidence.

Another way to learn humility is to serve others. Richard Foster reminds us that "more than any other single way, the grace of humility is worked into our lives through the Discipline of service."[14] Serving others, according to Foster, is, of all the classical spiritual disciplines, the "most conducive to the growth of humility." You should not be surprised by the connection between service and humility. One begets the other. Both benefit anyone other than yourself. Genuine service—an act initiated for the benefit of another hidden from an audience—will always lead to humility.

I am a volunteer police and fire chaplain for my city. I share this responsibility with five other men who give their time to serve our city's police officers and firefighters. We are most often called out to make death notifications or minister to relatives at the scene of a death, fire, or serious injury. Serving in this way leaves little room for self-centered pride. I am always humbled as I leave the home where a family member has taken his or her own life—and then return to the sleeping members of my own family. Service that takes you into the hurts of others will produce a humble spirit in you.

WAIT FOR GOD TO EXALT YOU

Waiting produces the patience we need if we are going to reach eternal goals. But not all waiting is the kind that produces patience. Let me describe three kinds of waiting.

Quiet waiting is like sitting on a porch at the end of the day, reflecting on the day's events.
This waiting takes you out of your tasks and goals to a place of quiet musing. It is a calculated pause to listen and learn. Quiet waiting results in a strong heart. King David knew that waiting on God produced this kind of strength. He penned the lyrics, "Wait for the Lord; be strong and take heart and wait for the Lord" (Ps. 27:14). Strength of heart, according to this mighty leader, came from waiting for God to work rather than going for it on your own.

"Just do it" is not a servant leader's mantra. God promised through his prophet Isaiah that "those who wait on the Lord will find new strength. They will fly high on wings like eagles. They will run and not grow weary. They will walk and not faint" (Isa. 40:31, NLT). Waiting upon the Lord renews a person's strength. Quiet waiting is a passive waiting. Your focus is listening for instruction on the next step while considering your last one.

Quiet waiting includes reflection. Warren Bennis observed that reflection is "a major way in which leaders learn from the past."[15] This practice helps the leader to say, "That's the way we will go." Bennis writes:

> Reflection may be the pivotal way we learn. Consider some of the ways of reflecting: looking back, thinking back, dreaming, journaling, talking it out, watching last week's game, asking for critiques, going on retreats—even telling jokes. Jokes are a way of making whatever-it-was understandable and acceptable.[16]

······························

QUIET REFLECTION GIVES THE LEADER
A TRANSCENDENT VIEW OF EVENTS
AND CHOICES.

······························

Quiet reflection gives the leader a transcendent view of events and choices. It provides a viewpoint that makes room for humor rather than worry.

Prayer is another way to wait quietly. Prayer puts all things earthly in perspective with things holy. Quiet prayer allows the searcher to meet her Guide and the disciple to know his Teacher. Prayer is "like farming," according to Robert Schuller. He offers these four steps to quiet prayer:

❖ In the first step, the soil must be broken, disked, and raked until it is prepared to receive the seed. In prayer, your soul must first be prepared by faith.

❖ Then the seed must be dropped. In Level Two prayer, your call for help must be raised.

❖ Then the weeds must be removed. In prayer, the negative elements in your thoughts and feelings must be eliminated like static on the line. You clear the channel and reprogram your mind with positive ideas and moods.

❖ And water must be supplied. In prayer, renewed vision, purpose, and enthusiasm must be added to your soul.[17]

Jesus practiced quiet waiting. Luke's story of Jesus describes him as a praying leader. He prayed all night before he chose his leadership team (Luke 6:12-16). Jesus was transfigured and his mission confirmed by God as he quietly prayed on a mountaintop with his three closest followers (Luke 9:28-36). His disciples asked him to teach them to pray after they had observed the power of prayer in his life (Luke 11:1-4). Quiet waiting through prayer and reflection was a core characteristic of Jesus' life.

Expectant waiting is like sitting in a restaurant waiting for a friend who said he would join you for breakfast. You wait expecting a promise to be kept. You wait with the certainty that your partner's word can be trusted. Spiritually, expectant waiting is trusting God's Word, knowing that he is up to something. You wait and expect something to happen, based upon his Word.

Jesus taught his disciples about expectant waiting. Before he ascended into heaven, he told them, "Do not leave Jerusalem, but wait for the gift my Father promised, which you have heard me speak about" (Acts 1:4). Jesus had been crucified, buried, and raised on the third day. Then he told his leadership team to go back to the scene of the crime and wait. They were to wait because in waiting they would receive "the gift [his] Father promised [them]." This is active waiting.

Quiet waiting is listening. Expectant waiting is looking! It is active and focused. The disciples waited for the promised Holy Spirit of God to pour out upon them. They had no idea what that gift would look, feel, taste, smell, or sound like. Their focus was the gift, not their circumstances. They waited based upon their trust in the One who told them to wait. Their waiting was filled with hope that what Jesus had told them would come true. Expectant waiting led to realized hope.

If you have ever waited through a pregnancy, you know what expectant waiting feels like. You know a birth is in the future, but you don't know when it will actually take place. You prepare. You get checkups. You pack the bags and keep the car filled with gas, and you wait. When the birth pains begin, you are ready to respond with joy and love. Expectant waiting is waiting for God to exalt you.

Frustrated waiting is like waiting in the doctor's office for two hours knowing you have work to do back at the office. The longer the wait, the greater the frustration. This kind of waiting leads to hurried decisions, loss of focus, and broken relationships.

Every time I have experienced frustrated waiting, I have made wrong decisions. When I lose trust in God's promises and people's word, I tend to start making things happen. My motives are frustration, not service. My results are defeat, not success.

You never see this kind of waiting with Jesus. He quietly and expectantly waited for God to accomplish his plan. A servant leader like Jesus waits on the prompting of his Master. Taking things into our own hands leads to confusion and loss of direction.

Waiting is neither procrastination nor indecision. These are born out of laziness and fear. Leaders cannot afford to procrastinate, and they can't hold up God's mission through their own indecision. But sometimes we are required to wait. Waiting in the context of Jesus' teachings is trusting that there is a season for everything (see Eccles. 3:1). It is staking your life on the reality that God makes things happen for his purposes and on his timetable. Waiting is trusting that "Timing (with a capital *T*) is everything."

JESUS HAD A SENSE OF TIMING

Jesus understood that the Father had ordained seasons in his life. This was part of what enabled him to wait as a leader. Jesus said several times during his ministry, "My time has not yet come." The first was when his mother told him they had run out of wine at the wedding feast in Cana. He said to her, "Dear woman, why do you involve me? . . . My time has not yet come" (John 2:4). On the night of Jesus' betrayal, John, the Gospel writer, records, "It was just before the Passover Feast. Jesus knew that the time had come for him to leave this world and go to the Father" (John 13:1). Jesus confessed to his Father that "the time [had] come" for his glorification (John 17:1). Jesus knew the importance of God's timing, especially for a leader with a mission.

Someone once said, "You cannot be impatient and humble." I believe this is true because impatience leads to reaction against events instead of waiting for divine direction. Impatience causes leaders to sacrifice insight for effort. It causes us to trust our natural instincts rather than God's work in our life.

IMPATIENT FOR GOD'S CALL

I am goal and task oriented. I am an achiever. "Keep moving" is one of my natural core values. I sensed God's call on my life to pastor when I was in high school. I went to college and seminary and served on the staff of a large suburban church as the minister to youth. At the age of thirty-three, I was serving as the executive director of a private foundation that owned and operated camps and conference centers in Colorado and Texas. I had been ordained and had earned my Ph.D. in New Testament studies. But I was not a pastor.

One day I sat quietly on the side of a mountain outside a Colorado camp. I opened my heart to God, praying, *Why haven't you let me be a pastor? I have my degrees and experience. I know I can do the job. Why haven't you let me do what I thought you called me to do sixteen years ago?* I was really upset. Then the still, small voice of the Spirit said, "Gene, you can be a postman and do what I called you to do." I listened longer. God's Spirit pointed out that the position I held had little to do with his call on my life. The Spirit continued, "Be faithful to the task at hand." I sensed that God knew how all this would work together for his good. Romans 8:28 came to mind. I realized that God was still at work in my life, molding me into the kind of pastor he wanted me to become. I learned that God's timing may not be our timing, but God's timing is always right. A year later I was interim pastor at the church I now have served as pastor for over ten years.

> IMPATIENCE LEADS TO REACTION
> AGAINST EVENTS INSTEAD OF WAITING
> FOR DIVINE DIRECTION. IMPATIENCE
> CAUSES LEADERS TO SACRIFICE
> INSIGHT FOR EFFORT.

You may be waiting on God's timing in your life. You may feel that what you are doing now has nothing to do with God's call on your life or the mission God has called you to complete. Be patient. Wait. Find a quiet hill or field where you can sit still and hear the voice of God. You will soon discover that if you pay attention to God's timing in your present, you will see God's timing in your future.

Humility and waiting are part of a servant leader's lifestyle. A godly confidence combined with trusting patience allows the servant leader to carry out the mission of God in his life. Humility and patience equip him or her to carry out lifelong purposes.

A FIRST STEP—AND A CRUCIAL CHOICE

How does a person follow Jesus' teachings and example if his words are so counter to our natural habits? What do you do to put these truths into your life?

You cannot apply this first principle of a servant leader to your life unless you commit yourself to follow Jesus. You must decide if you will design your life after the pattern of Jesus or design your life around the best thinking and experience the world has to offer. You must answer the question "Who is master of my life?"

Here's why your answer to that question is basic to this study: No one can be a servant without a master. You cannot be a servant leader as modeled by Jesus without having him as your

Master. Jesus said you can't serve two masters. You will either hate the one and love the other, or you will be devoted to one and despise the other (Matt. 6:24). Remember, *God* is spelled E-G-O or G-O-D. You choose. I offer to you that leaders without Jesus as their Master can serve only themselves, no matter how they might imagine that they are being great servants to humanity and to their ideals.

Take a moment to examine your heart and answer the following questions:

- ❖ Have I confessed my self-centeredness that leads to sin and resistance to God's leadership in my life?

- ❖ Have I confessed that Jesus is Master of my life? *Romans 10:9*

- ❖ Do I live my life as if I am in control or as if Christ is in control? *Galatians 2:20*

- ❖ Have I shown a willingness to humble myself before others, or am I happier when I earn a seat at a head table?

The answers to these questions describe your relationship with Jesus Christ. The rest of this book will only be an exercise in self-will if Christ is not in control of every aspect of your life. If you want to settle this issue in your life right now, pause and ask Christ to be Savior and, just as important, Lord of your life. When you have done that, call a friend or pastor and ask him or her to join you in prayer. Real servant leadership begins when you decide to learn from and follow the real Servant Leader, Jesus Christ.

SOMEONE LIKE YOU

Bob Buford, chairman and CEO of Buford Television and founder of Leadership Network, tells how he came to a "halftime" in his life.[18] He was a successful businessman with a great wife and

family, but he had begun to seek significance beyond his accumu-
lated success. During those days of self-evaluation, Bob received a
call from his brother saying Bob's son, Ross, was missing on the
Rio Grande. Bob tells the painful story of how he waited to hear
of his son's recovery. While waiting for the rescuers to find his
son, Bob said he walked to a limestone bluff overlooking the river
that later he would learn had taken his son's life. He remembers
saying to himself:

> Here's something you can't dream your way out of. Here's
> something you can't think your way out of, buy your way
> out of, or work your way out of. . . . This is . . . something
> you can only trust your way out of.[19]

Bob Buford lost his son. That event, along with the unset-
tling that had already begun in his life, set Bob on a journey that
would change his life forever and influence the lives of many
others. That halftime in Bob's life resulted in the Leadership
Network, a privately funded organization dedicated to developing Christian leaders in the church for the twenty-first century.
Many church leaders, paid staff and lay leaders, have benefited
from Bob Buford's new direction in life that resulted from his
halftime in the game of life. It all began when he decided he must
trust his way out of where he was.

This book can be the beginning of a halftime in your life, a
time when you evaluate how you lead and who you are in relationship with the Servant Leader, Jesus. The time you spend
walking through these pages can launch you into new experiences in life that you have never imagined. You and many others
can benefit from who you will become after spending time following the Leader.

The first principle of servant leadership is "servant leaders
humble themselves and wait for God to exalt them." This principle

does not come naturally to you. It is learned and nurtured over a lifetime. These traits, however, are essential to becoming a leader after the model and teachings of Jesus. You have begun a journey that will slowly change your heart and how you lead others. It is a lifelong journey that will often challenge conventional wisdom and your natural instincts. This journey is the kind you can only "trust your way out of." But, isn't that the kind of trip you would rather be on anyway?

FOR STUDY AND REFLECTION

- When you think of the concept of humility, what pictures first come to your mind? What are your concerns about being known as a humble person?

- List ways you can translate Jesus' teaching to "take a seat in the back" into your daily life. Is this really possible where you live?

- How does Jesus' example in Philippians 2 help you understand humility as a way of life?

- Based on your understanding of this chapter, what role does pride play in the life of a servant leader?

- Describe your feelings about the concept of "waiting for God to exalt you." List some examples from this chapter and your own life that would confirm this principle.

- Share examples from your life of when you experienced quiet waiting, expectant waiting, and/or frustrated waiting. What did you learn during those times?

- Summarize your understanding of the first principle of servant leadership. List three ways you can apply this principle to your leadership issues this week.

Endnotes for Principle #1

1. Bill Hybels, *Descending into Greatness* (Grand Rapids: Zondervan, 1993), 16.

2. Ibid.

3. Robert Sterling and Gene Wilkes. "Riches to Rags," in the musical *We Beheld His Glory* (Los Angeles: Warner/Chapel Music, Inc., 1987).

4. Henri J. M. Nouwen, *In the Name of Jesus, Reflections on Christian Leadership* (New York: Crossroad, 1989), 62–3.

5. Peter F. Drucker, *Managing the Non-Profit Organization* (New York: HarperCollins, 1990), 20.

6. Max DePree, *Leadership Jazz* (New York: Doubleday, 1992), 172–3.

7. Warren Bennis, *Why Leaders Can't Lead* (San Francisco: Jossey-Bass, 1989), 117–18.

8. Anthony DeMello, *The Song of the Bird,* 2d ed. (Anand, India: Gujarat Sahitya Prakash, 1982), 129.

9. Anthony Campolo, *Seven Deadly Sins* (Colorado Springs: Victor, 1987), 74.

10. Ken Blanchard, *We Are the Beloved* (Grand Rapids: Zondervan, 1994), 43.

11. Ibid.

12. Proverbs 16:5, 18, 19.

13. Brennan Manning, *The Signature of Jesus* (Sisters, Oreg.: Multnomah, 1996), 141.

14. Richard J. Foster, *Celebration of Discipline,* rev. and enl. (New York: HarperCollins, 1988), 130.

15. Warren Bennis, *On Becoming a Leader* (Reading, Mass.: Addison-Wesley Publishing, 1994), 114.

16. Ibid., 115.

17. Robert H. Schuller, *Prayer: My Soul's Adventure with God* (Nashville: Nelson, 1995), 141.

18. Bob Buford, *Halftime* (Grand Rapids: Zondervan, 1994).

19. Ibid., 56.

FIRST BE A FOLLOWER

IN THE twenty-first-century organization, all leaders
must learn to follow if they are to successfully lead.
DOUGLAS K. SMITH *The Leader of the Future*

ALL leaders are actual or potential power holders,
but not all power holders are leaders.
JAMES M. BURNS *Leadership*

THE BIBLE says comparatively little about leadership
and a great deal about followership. Jesus did not
invite Peter, Andrew, James, and John to become
leaders immediately. He said, "Follow Me."
LEITH ANDERSON *A Church for the
Twenty-First Century*

A PERSON can be assigned, selected,
or designated for a position, but a person
cannot be appointed to leadership.
LOVETT H. WEEMS JR. *Church Leadership*

LEADERS both "lead" and "follow"
in permission-giving churches.
WILLIAM M. EASUM *Sacred Cows
Make Gourmet Burgers*

MY OLDEST daughter is somewhat of a daredevil. She came home from a youth-group outing one day with a huge smile on her face. She told us she had strapped herself into one of those ninety-foot swings along with two of the sponsors and taken the ride of her life!

Her mother and I responded with the most famous of parental responses: "You what?!" She promised pictures to prove it. Pictures would not be necessary, we said. Her mother asked, "What's gotten into you? How could you risk your life like that?" I asked, "Do you really go seventy miles per hour at the bottom of the swing?" We were filled with both fear and amazement at our daughter's choices.

Jesus' parents had the same reactions to one of his decisions. When he was twelve, he decided to stay in Jerusalem and discuss the Scriptures with the religious leaders while his parents headed home with friends and family. The Bible says that when they saw him in the temple, "they were astonished" (Luke 2:48). Any parent would be somewhat amazed to find a twelve-year-old boy in a Bible study at church instead of on a trip with friends. Mary, Jesus' mother, went into parental mode when she asked, "Son, why have you treated us like this? Your father and I have been anxiously searching for you." No word from Joseph. He must have been pondering his son's desire to sit among his elders and discuss the Word of God. The parents of Jesus responded with concern and amazement at their son's choice to stay behind and be about his Father's business.

I believe this event at the temple and others like it prepared Jesus for the responses he would get the rest of his life to the radical decisions he would make. By the time Jesus began leading his group of followers to complete his mission, he was no doubt accustomed to people's responses to his choices.

People showed a wide range of reactions to Jesus. Some were amazed. Others could not believe he could be so foolish. Others hated him. Leaders, I have learned, must be comfortable with how others may respond to their decisions.

JESUS LED SO THAT OTHERS COULD BE FOLLOWERS

LET'S drop into Jesus' life at the point of his decision to lead his followers to Jerusalem. Mark 10:32 tells us that Jesus was "leading" his followers toward the city. The word used for "lead" here means to go before a group. Jesus was out in front of his followers, showing the way. Mark said that the disciples, the twelve closest to Jesus, "were astonished" at his decision to go to Jerusalem. The word can also be translated "marveled." Why did his closest followers marvel at this decision?

By this time in Jesus' ministry, opposition to his mission had grown considerably. The disciples had seen heated exchanges between Jesus and religious leaders. They must have wondered why Jesus wanted to stir up a hornet's nest again by going to denominational headquarters in Jerusalem. The disciples may have marveled by saying, "I can't believe he's doing this. He's going to get us all killed." They also may have said, "You've got to give the guy credit. He's got nerve to go back there." Leaders make bold decisions. Those who follow are either amazed or afraid.

....

**FEAR IS OFTEN A BY-PRODUCT
OF THOSE WHO SEE THEIR LEADER
AS A PROVIDER ONLY.**

....

Mark also tells us that the other followers—besides the Twelve—were afraid. Why? This group also knew of the potential showdown in Jerusalem. They must have feared a fatal resolution to the conflict between Jesus and their religious leaders. These people were those who followed Jesus because he had fed them or healed them. His great teachings gave them hope. His compassion for the lost motivated them to love others. Jesus was a leader who inspired their hearts and supplied their needs. Losing Jesus in Jerusalem would mean losing a leader who filled emotional as well as physical needs. They did not want their leader to risk their well-being for the sake of his mission. *Fear is often a by-product of those who see their leader as a provider only.*

JESUS STATED HIS INTENTIONS.
GOOD LEADERS DO.

As the leader, Jesus also made his intentions clear. When he saw their reactions, he pulled the Twelve aside and explained what was about to happen. Good leaders state their intentions to those closest to them. Max DePree says that the first responsibility of the leader is to define reality.[1] Jesus defined the reality of his mission as he told his followers the truth once again: He would go to the great city and be betrayed and condemned by the religious leaders. The religious leaders, in turn, would turn him over to the Romans, who would torture and kill him. On the third day, however, he would be raised from the grave. To his closest followers, Jesus laid out how he saw the future.

Jesus' stating his intentions to go to Jerusalem and die and be raised on the third day was one way he painted the vision for his disciples. Remember, vision is simply what the mission looks like when it is complete. Vision is a picture of the future that the leader paints for those who follow him. Jesus' earthly mission to "give his life as a ransom for many" (Mark 10:45) was complete when he died on the cross. This is why he said, "It is finished" (John 19:30), as he died. His eternal mission continued as he was raised from the dead and eventually took his place at the right hand of the Father. Jesus knew what the end of his mission looked like, and he wanted his followers to know this before it happened.

Let me pause here and say that Jesus knew this was about to happen because of his complete divinity. God sees the past, present, and future at the same moment. Jesus had an advantage over us mere mortals in that he could see the future. On the other hand, as fully human, he was intuitive enough to know that returning to Jerusalem at this time spelled the end of his earthly ministry. Too many signs pointed in that direction. The question, then, may be, "Why go if you know that is what is going to happen?" As we observe Jesus' life and ministry, we will see that he knew his mission and trusted the Father's timing to the point that, when he sensed that both had come together, he acted. Jesus sensed that his return to Jerusalem was necessary to complete the Father's plan for his life.

....

GOOD LEADERS CULTIVATE THE ABILITY
TO READ CURRENT EVENTS AND THUS
HAVE A STRONG SENSE OF WHAT
THE FUTURE MAY BRING.

....

Although Jesus had the supernatural ability to see the future, I believe good leaders cultivate the ability to read current events and thus have a strong sense of what the future may bring. Great leaders take present circumstances and spell out potential scenarios from those factors. They seem to see what no one else can see. Bennis affirms the role of intuition in leadership when he writes:

> A part of whole-brain thinking includes learning to trust what Emerson called the "blessed impulse," the hunch, the vision that shows you in a flash the absolutely right thing to do. Everyone has these visions; leaders learn to trust them.[2]

Leaders trust their hunches about the outcome of current events. Then they act on those hunches. And they keep their followers informed, even when such information invites mixed reactions, as it did when Jesus foretold the Jerusalem events.

I was accused of many things as I led our church to make changes in its structure and style so that we could reach more people. The accusation that amused me most and pleased me at the same time was that I had "an agenda." Having an agenda in the midst of change seemed for some to rank up there with embezzlement and adultery. During one rather heated discussion, one church member was standing near a marker board, and he said, "You want to know your problem?" I said, "Not really, but go ahead." He walked to the board, picked up a marker, and wrote in all caps: *AGENDA*. "You have an agenda!" he proclaimed. I think he expected to surprise me by exposing my secret. He must have waited for me to turn red faced because he had caught me with my hand in the cookie jar. But I could only smile. I thanked him for noticing! I had been trying to spell out my agenda for over a year. I was happy that someone had caught on.

Every leader has an agenda—the ultimate mission she has been called to. When others begin to see that agenda, the leader has done her job! When she states her intentions clearly, she gives followers the opportunity to accept the plans or seek to end them.

Jesus had an agenda: to lay down his life as a ransom for many. Going to Jerusalem was part of that agenda. This was not some benign policy statement; it was a decision that actually caused fear and amazement. We shouldn't be surprised when God's calling leads to this. The people we lead are much better off understanding what the "agenda" is.

WHEN LEADERS DECIDE, OTHERS MAKE CHOICES TOO

As soon as Jesus told his disciples of his intentions, two of them moved in to take advantage of the situation. James and John were among Jesus' closest followers. He had called them very early in his public mission to be part of the Twelve. They were brothers in a family fishing business. Their nickname was Sons of Thunder. They must have been in some pretty big brawls to gain that kind of reputation! When Jesus told them to follow him so he could show them how to catch people for God rather than fish for themselves, they dropped their nets and followed him. Jesus consistently chose James and John to share his deepest concerns and joys with. By the time of Jesus' decision to go to Jerusalem, James and John had seen Jesus perform miracles and had been with him at Peter's confession in Caesarea Philippi and on the mountain of his transfiguration. They had a strong relationship with their leader.

The telltale sign of their relationship with Jesus was James and John's request: "We want you to do for us whatever we ask" (Mark 10:35). Some people may be appalled at the audacity of these men to approach Jesus with such an attitude. Surely they were too comfortable with their leader. Where was their respect? Why didn't Jesus scold them for their presumption?

People can follow when the leader establishes trust.
I believe their request revealed the open and genuine relationship Jesus shared with his followers. The brothers were simply
acting out what Jesus had taught them about God's desire to
hear the requests of those who love him: "You may ask me for
anything in my name, and I will do it" (John 14:14). James and
John trusted Jesus and approached him with their heartfelt
request.

Jesus answered with, "What do you want me to do for you?"
(Mark 10:36). Servant leaders accept the honest requests of
those they serve. Jesus did not scold. He did not roll his eyes.
He wanted to understand their request before he responded to
them. Jesus responded to James and John the way the authors of
Managing from the Heart suggest that caring managers respond
to those who work with them. The authors offer the first two
"requests everyone at work makes of you":

> Please don't make me wrong, even if you disagree.
> Hear and understand me.[3]

Jesus did not put James and John down for their request,
although it was off base. He did not "make them wrong" by his
attitude toward them. Jesus waited to understand what they
wanted from him.

Jesus built the kind of relationship with James and John
that allowed for this kind of request and patient understanding.
Relationship is everything in leadership. Burns notes that
leadership is first relational.[4] Leaders lead most effectively
when relationships are open and strong between them and
their followers.

How do you have that kind of relationship with your followers? One word: *trust*. Stephen R. Covey has developed a
"Principle-Centered Leadership Paradigm" with four levels

and key principles.[5] People are the "highest value [in this paradigm] because they are the programmers—they produce everything else at the personal, interpersonal, managerial, and organizational levels." The key principle in this level is trust.

> Trust is the foundation of all effective relationships and organizations. Without a culture of high trust, true empowerment can neither be established nor sustained. Why, then, is the trust level in most organizations so chronically low? The reason is that trust is not the result of organizational imperative or program. In other words, it is not a quick fix. It is the fruit of trustworthiness at the personal level.[6]

Max DePree explains that building trust in organizations "has become a chief responsibility of leaders, an essential duty especially in the eyes of the followers."[7] Warren Bennis claims that trust is one of six basic ingredients of leadership. "Integrity is the basis of *trust,* which is not so much an ingredient of leadership as it is a product. It is the one quality that cannot be acquired, but must be earned. It is given by coworkers and followers, and without it, the leader can't function."[8] Trust is the foundation upon which relationships in every setting are built.

Jesus' trustworthiness at the personal level of his relationship with James and John allowed them to trust that he would openly consider their request of him. This principle of trust is essential in churches. Bill Easum has observed that trust is a key element in his paradigm of permission-giving churches. "Trust and love are at the heart of permission-giving churches. Love lets go and permits the other to stretch his or her wings. Trust operates on mutual respect."[9]

Trust between a church leader and members of the church

allows the work of mission to be done. Trust destroys an atmosphere of control and creates an air of freedom. Trust allows the leader to lead.

People can follow when their view of leadership is corrected.

James and John had enough savvy to know that when Jesus announced his intentions to go to Jerusalem, the Messiah's work to build the kingdom of God was almost complete. We've got to give them credit for hearing Jesus' announcement and then trusting him enough to want to be part of the action. Unlike Peter, who scolded Jesus for telling of his suffering, James and John looked beyond those events to when Jesus would sit on the throne of the new kingdom. Peter missed the kind of Messiah Jesus would be. James and John missed the kind of throne he would sit upon. Both misconceptions required correction from their Lord.

James and John sensed that something important would happen in Jerusalem. The Sons of Thunder asked, "Let one of us sit at your right and the other at your left in your glory" (Mark 10:37). Their request reveals a common misconception about leadership: We think that if we have the position, then we have the power to lead. James and John believed the myth that a place of power in the kingdom meant a position of leadership in the kingdom.

Just because you have a position of leadership does not mean you are a leader. We ambitiously long for the corner office. We think if we get there, then people will listen to us. The reality is that if people do not listen to you now, they will not listen to you when you "arrive." But the misconception remains.

James and John understood that in any kingdom, the places closest to the king had to have more power and prestige attached to them. That's how the Romans did it. That is how the leadership of Israel did it. Positions near the top are where you want to be when the king comes to power. This worldview, however, breeds competition rather than cooperation.

We are competitive people. As I sit writing this paragraph, I watch three boys running outside my hotel room in North Carolina. A woman, presumably a mother of at least one of the boys, times each child as he runs from the edge of a sidewalk to a tree and back. Each boy jumps for joy or cringes after his time is called out. He wants to have the fastest time. Without hearing a word, I can tell who has beaten the other times by the runners' body language. My mind travels back to the days I raced friends on playgrounds or in backyards. I mostly cringed at the end of my races!

....

AS LONG AS POSITION IS HONORED
ABOVE DISCIPLESHIP, CHURCH LEADERS
WILL HONOR THE AMBITIOUS OVER
THE OBEDIENT.

....

There is nothing wrong with competition; it has helped make the United States an economic and military power in this world. The problem comes when we declare one's value solely upon his or her time in the grass races! One of those boys will walk away from that self-made track a winner because he had the best time. If the mother does her job, all three will leave feeling valuable because they have raced.

Confusion arises when you equate higher positions with leadership—especially when it comes to the things of God. While position can present opportunities for leadership, position does not guarantee that you are a leader. But as long as position is honored above discipleship—being a follower—church leaders will honor the ambitious over the obedient.

JESUS WANTED HIS DISCIPLES
TO BE FOLLOWERS FIRST

Jesus gently exposed his followers' misconception about leadership in the kingdom by making a statement and asking two questions. First he said, "You don't know what you are asking" (Mark 10:38). Jesus knew what comprised his path to glory. He knew what the end of his mission looked like. He had no intentions of holding any position within an earthly paradigm of power. His only goal was to bring glory to his Father in heaven by completing his mission as Suffering Servant Messiah. He knew that his road to his throne included betrayal, mockery, torture, and death. He also knew he would be raised to life on the third day after his death. Jesus' statement to James and John showed that they did not grasp the reality of their leader's mission and, ultimately, their mission.

AMBITION IS NOT THE SAME THING
AS WILLINGNESS TO FOLLOW
JESUS TO THE CROSS.

Jesus asked James and John a question that exposed their ambitious hearts and misconceptions about kingdom leadership. Jesus couched his question in language of that day. He asked, "Can you drink the cup I drink or be baptized with the baptism I am baptized with?" (Mark 10:38). Jesus was referring to his suffering and death by this question. The cup was an Old Testament symbol for suffering. Jesus used this image of suffering in the Garden of Gethsemane on the night he was betrayed. He asked his Father in heaven, "Take this cup [of suffering on the cross] from me" (Mark 14:36). He asked if there was any other way to lay down his life as a ransom. He had seen too many crucifixions in his short lifetime. He wanted no part of that. However, he humbled himself to follow the will of his Father rather than carrying out the desires of his heart when he prayed, "Yet not what I will, but what you will" (Mark 14:36).

Baptism was also a biblical picture of suffering. Jesus told his disciples at another time, "But I have a baptism to undergo, and how distressed I am until it is completed!" (Luke 12:50). You have heard of a baptism by fire. It's how you train the new person in the office! One picture of suffering is that of being immersed in pain. Jesus asked his ambitious followers if they were ready to go through the humiliation of suffering before they were rewarded a place beside him in his kingdom.

Jesus was more interested in his disciples' willingness to follow him to the cross than in their ambition to hold places of power in his kingdom. Ambition is not the same thing as willingness to follow Jesus to the cross. Jesus cared that his followers were willing to obey him.

FIRST A FOLLOWER: ARE YOU?

JESUS' response to James and John is the basis for our second principle of servant leadership:

> *Servant leaders follow Jesus rather than seek a position.*

Jesus wants servant leaders to be followers first. Contemporary observers of leadership also acknowledge the need for a leader to be a follower. Douglas K. Smith has written,

> In the twenty-first-century organization, all leaders must learn to follow if they are to successfully lead. . . . Leaders at all levels and in all situations must pay close attention to situations in which their most effective option is to follow—not because the hierarchy demands they "obey," but because performance requires them to rely on the capacities and insights of other people.[10]

Max DePree claims that becoming a good follower is important training to become a good leader. "If one is already a leader," he writes, "the lessons of following are especially appropriate. Leaders understand the essential contributions as well as the limitations of good followers."[11] Leaders must know the skills of following if they are to contribute most to those seeking to reach the goal with them.

Following is at the core of being a servant leader. The word *disciple* means "learner." In Jesus' day, disciples literally followed their teacher around as they learned from him. To learn from Jesus means to follow Jesus. The church today seems to be more interested in those who are ambitious to lead than in those who are willing to follow. Leith Anderson makes this observation about the church's obsession with leadership when the overwhelming emphasis in Scripture is about following:

> It should surprise us that so much is said about leaders and so little about followers, especially among Christians committed to the Bible. The Bible says comparatively little about leadership and a great deal about followership. Jesus did not invite Peter, Andrew, James, and John to become leaders immediately. He said, "Follow Me."[12]

Jesus called his disciples to follow him. They became leaders only after Jesus empowered them to lead; he empowered them by insisting they follow him first.

WHAT MISSION IS TO FOLLOWING

Leadership begins with mission. Without mission there is no need or motivation to lead. A God-sized mission that captures the heart of a person draws him into leadership because he must have others involved in order to carry out a mission of that size. I believe God never calls his people to do something they can do on their own. Otherwise, they would not need God!

> LEADERSHIP BEGINS WITH MISSION.
> WITHOUT MISSION THERE IS NO NEED
> OR MOTIVATION TO LEAD.

Biblical leadership always begins with a God-sized mission in the form of a call by God. Those commissioned by God to carry out that call become leaders because they first follow God's call. *Biblical servant leadership never begins with the individual's wishes to better the world or attain a personal goal.* Servant leadership finds its motive from God's commissioning a person to carry out a divine plan among a group of people. Becoming servant to the mission and a follower of the God who called you is the heart of servant leadership.

Here are some familiar examples from the Bible to illustrate:

❖ Joseph became a leader after God placed a vision in his heart to preserve his covenant people.

❖ Moses became a servant leader of God when he followed God's call on his life to go to Pharaoh and deliver the message: "The Lord says, Let my people go."

❖ Gideon would never have been a leader if he had not followed God's mission to deliver the tribes of Israel from the Midianites.

❖ David became a king when God, through Samuel, anointed him king. He humbly followed God's plan to assume the throne of Israel. He did not seek it.

❖ Isaiah became a prophet leader when God called him to take a message of hope and judgment to the people of Israel.

❖ Nehemiah became a remarkable leader when God commissioned him to rebuild the wall around Jerusalem.

❖ Esther became a leader when God, through Mordecai, called her to stand before the king to protect the remnant of God's people.

❖ Peter became a leader in the early church after Jesus commissioned him and the other disciples to make disciples of all peoples.

❖ The apostle Paul led from a clear mission to extend the boundaries of God's grace to those outside the Jewish faith.

I believe you can walk through the Bible and illustrate that leadership among God's people began with God's call and that person's willingness to follow. Leaders among God's people come into leadership *as they are carrying out* God's mission/call. They do not seek positions of leadership so that they can do great things. Do you truly see the difference between these two approaches? Many, many would-be leaders have never seen the difference. Rather than committing themselves to following God's call and plan, they commit themselves to getting into a position where they will have the money they need and the power they need to carry out their vision of God's work in the world. We have too many leaders of the latter sort. We can only wonder what God might have done with those leaders if they had simply followed his call and left position, power, and money out of the equation.

Rick Warren, the pastor of Saddleback Community Church, is a contemporary example of a servant leader who is first a follower of God's mission in his life. Rick began his ministry in south Orange County because God called him to build a church around the mission of God as spelled out in a great commitment to the great commandment and the great commission. Rick has followed God's call and has become servant to the mission God gave him. He now is leader of thousands of people who are Saddleback Church and many other church leaders because of his willingness and humble service toward carrying out what God has commissioned. Warren's incredibly popular and insightful book, *The Purpose-Driven Church,* describes the power of purpose or mission in a church and a church leader's life. He makes this essential point: "Nothing precedes purpose. The starting point for every church should be the question, 'Why do we exist?' Until you know what your church exists for, you have no foundation, no motivation, and no direction for ministry."[13] Throughout his book, Rick explains the role of the leader as he guides people to discover, articulate, and build processes to live out divine purposes through the church.

I believe that God is using men and women with Rick Warren's heart and vision to call the church back to its core purposes to revive and reform the church for a new work in this culture. God is looking for servant leaders who are first followers of God's mission in their own lives to lead these purposeful churches. Only purpose-driven pastors can lead purpose-driven churches.

TO FOLLOW MEANS TO OBEY, NOT WRITE OUR OWN TICKET

James and John naively answered Jesus' questions with, "Sure! Why not?" They'd agree to anything to have the chance to rule with the king. They overlooked the suffering of servant leadership, however, for the luxuries of a position in the kingdom.

Before you judge the Sons of Thunder, remember that we are very much like them. We, too, want places up front when Jesus defeats his enemies. We forget that suffering with Jesus comes before reigning with Jesus. Jesus wanted James and John to know that following him would cost them their lives.

JESUS TEACHES THAT WE LEARN TO LEAD
BY LEARNING TO FOLLOW.

Too many times we who are ambitious to lead agree to whatever it takes to acquire a place of leadership. We naturally pursue places of power so we can command others and share the perks of position. But Jesus' teachings on servant leadership do not support such human efforts and desires. Jesus teaches that we learn to lead by learning to follow.

Calvin Miller has noted that servant leadership "is nurtured in the Spirit by following Jesus. Servant leaders generally are created not in commanding others but in *obeying* their Commander. In such a mystique, executive arrogance is not possible. The yielded leader is always an incarnation of Christ, the real leader of His church."[14] The key concept in Miller's observation is "obeying." Now there's an idea that has lost its place in a post-Christian culture! Obedience is to the nineties what restraint was to the eighties: the concept is laughable given current conditions! Obedience, however, is the basis for following Jesus.

A root concept for the verb *obey* in the two biblical languages and Latin is "to listen."[15] Henri Nouwen and his coauthors observed this about Jesus' life:

> Obedience, as it is embodied in Jesus Christ, is a total listening, a giving attention with no hesitation or limitation, a being "all ear." . . . When used by Jesus, the word *obedience* has no association with fear, but rather is the expression of his most intimate, loving relationship. Jesus' actions and words are the obedient response to this love of his Father.[16]

Obedience begins with listening to—not just hearing—the words of another. Action is the response of obedience. Jesus responded in obedience to his Father because of his love for his Father. Servant leaders respond to God in obedience because of their love for God. For, after listening, you are obedient when you do what you have heard. For example, children are obedient when they do what their parents ask them to do. A child is not obedient by simply saying he will clean up his room. He is obedient when his socks are in the drawer.

Obedience is simply translating what you hear into action. To be a follower first, you must be willing to obey whoever is leading you. Successful followers translate what they hear from their leader into actions that serve the mission they share. Obedience is not an act of subservience to a dictator; it is an act of love and respect. Jesus said he would know how much you and I love him by the way we obey (do) his commandments (John 15:10, 14). To obey someone is to show respect and love toward them.

Servant leadership in the kingdom is not about seeking position and power. It is about following Jesus as he serves others and suffers on their behalf. Servant leaders follow Jesus by doing what he says to do first in whatever context they find themselves. Servant leadership may require drinking the cup and being baptized with the baptism of Christ's suffering (Mark 10:38-39).

HOW DO I KNOW IF I'M A FOLLOWER FIRST?

Following Jesus is like humbling yourself before God; neither is a natural act. We tend to get control of our lives, set goals, and go for them without paying attention to the things of God. We have already talked about ways we can humble ourselves, but how can we be certain we are following Jesus rather than seeking a position? Here are some steps that can help us answer that question.

First, simply put yourself in James and John's sandals. Get into the context of their situation, and seek to understand why they approached Jesus. One way to do this is to complete the statement: "I am like James and John because _____ _____." Your answer may differ from mine, but I am like the Sons of Thunder because I want a place next to Jesus in the kingdom without suffering what it takes to be there. My ambition for a place next to Jesus in his kingdom outweighs my desire to follow Jesus to the cross.

A second way to see if you are following Jesus first is to make a list of your ambitions, those things that drive you to accomplish all you do and to acquire all you have. What gets you up in the morning? What keeps you in the office or school beyond normal hours? Are recognition, power, and authority on your list? You may be seeking security, acceptance, and lack of conflict in your life. This list of what you are seeking can help point to your heart's desires and what truly drives you to do what you are doing.

A third exercise is to identify God's call on your life. Answer the question: "What has God called me to do? What specifically has God told me to do with my life?" God's call may be to build a strong family or to live out the great commandment in the marketplace. Don't get hung up in the details. Those are spelled out in the Bible. God's call certainly is for you to be a follower of Jesus wherever you find yourself. If you have not taken time to discover God's call on your life, I recommend books like Bob Buford's *Game Plan*[17] or Bob Shank's *Total Life Management*[18] as guides for helping you discover God's unique purpose for you.

A final way to test your ability to follow first is to ask yourself, "What am I doing to obey Christ's call to mission in my life? Do my actions reflect what I have heard God tell me to do?" If you are on mission to build Christ's church, what are you doing to purposefully build the church? If you are on mission to build a business around the purposes of God in your life, what are you doing to show your employees and customers that mission? If

God has called you to build a strong family, what have you done today to actually build up your family? What you do tells you—and others—what you really believe.

Being a servant leader begins by following Jesus rather than pursuing your ambitions. Pause now, and prayerfully consider the questions above. Your answers will help you know where you are on the path of becoming a servant leader.

FOR STUDY AND REFLECTION

- Would you consider yourself a follower or a leader? List the advantages of being a follower. List the disadvantages. List the advantages of being a leader. List the disadvantages.

- Has anyone ever accused you of having an agenda? If so, what was it? Could you say that your agenda was the same as your vision for your life?

- How are you like James and John? In what ways are you not like these two position seekers?

- List examples of where you see "position equals power to lead" in the organizations to which you belong.

- Jesus tested James's and John's hearts by asking if they were willing to follow him to the cross. They said, "Sure!" What would your response be?

- Agree or disagree with the statement "Without mission there is no need or motivation to lead." Give examples to support your position.

- Write the second principle of servant leadership in your own words. List three ways you can apply this principle to your leadership issues this week.

Endnotes for Principle #2

1. Max DePree, *Leadership Is an Art* (New York: Doubleday, 1989), 9.

2. Warren Bennis, *On Becoming a Leader* (San Francisco: Jossey-Bass, 1989), 104.

3. Hyler Bracey, et al., *Managing from the Heart* (New York: Dell, 1990), 11–12. You can demonstrate how Jesus lived out the other three requests, too. They are: 3. Tell me the truth with compassion. 4. Remember to look for my loving intentions. 5. Acknowledge the greatness within me.

4. Burns, James MacGregor, *Leadership* (New York: Harper & Row, 1978), 18.

5. Stephen R. Covey, *Principle-Centered Leadership* (New York: Simon and Schuster, 1992), 181–9.

6. Ibid., 182–3.

7. Max DePree, *Leading without Power* (San Francisco: Jossey-Bass, 1997), 134.

8. Warren Bennis, *On Becoming a Leader,* 41. See also 164–7.

9. Bill Easum, *Sacred Cows Make Great Burgers* (Nashville: Abingdon, 1995), 51.

10. Douglas K. Smith, "The Following Part of Leading" in *The Leader of the Future,* ed. by Frances Hesselbein, Marshall Goldsmith, and Richard Beckhard (San Francisco: Jossey-Bass, 1997), 199–200.

11. Max DePree, *Leadership Jazz* (New York: Doubleday, 1992), 198.

12. Leith Anderson, *A Church for the Twenty-First Century* (Minneapolis: Bethany, 1992), 222.

13. Rick Warren, *The Purpose-Driven Church* (Grand Rapids: Zondervan, 1995), 81.

14. Calvin Miller, *The Empowered Leader* (Nashville: Broadman & Holman, 1995), 17. Italics mine.

15. Donald P. McNeill, Douglas A. Morrison, Henri J. M. Nouwen, *Compassion: A Reflection on the Christian Life* (New York: Doubleday, 1983), 36.

16. Ibid., 36–7.

17. Bob Buford, *Game Plan* (Grand Rapids: Zondervan, 1997).

18. Bob Shank, *Total Life Management* (Sisters, Oreg.: Multnomah, 1990).

FIND GREATNESS
IN SERVICE

KEEP your eyes on the task, not on yourself.
The task matters, and you are a servant.
PETER DRUCKER *Managing the
Non-Profit Organization*

[SHEPHERD] is not a figure of strong over weak
or "lords" over servants. Quite the contrary. The
shepherd figure is one of love, service, and openness.
LYNN ANDERSON *They Smell Like Sheep*

POWER, for the sake of lording it over fellow-creatures
or adding to personal pomp, is rightly judged base.
WINSTON CHURCHILL in *Churchill on Leadership*

WHOEVER wants to become great among
you must be your servant, and whoever
wants to be first must be your slave.
JESUS *Matthew 20:26-27*

AFTER Jesus corrected the thinking of James and John, his job as leader was not over. The work of leadership is not complete until the mission is accomplished. Before that, leadership is a 24-7 job. When the two brothers' request got back to the other ten disciples, a turf war broke out. The ten did not like James and John's getting in front of them to receive recognition when Jesus' kingdom was set up. Their ongoing who's-the-greatest argument turned into a who-gets-the-best-seats argument.

When Jesus heard the noise, he called his leadership team together to lay down the ground rules—again. Here's what he said:

> *You know that those who are regarded as rulers of the Gentiles lord it over them, and their high officials exercise authority over them. Not so with you. Instead, whoever wants to become great among you must be your servant, and whoever wants to be first must be slave of all. For even the Son of Man did not come to be served, but to serve, and to give his life as a ransom for many.*   Mark 10:42-45

These words are Jesus' most clear yet most avoided teachings on leadership. His words are almost never quoted when the discussion turns to leadership. Few conferences invite potential or actual leaders to begin with this description of a leader when building a personal leadership style. We tend to either read over his blatant message or, at best, use the passage as illustrative material in a call to service.

Jesus redefined the vocabulary of leadership among God's people when he spoke to his disciples that day. Let's take Jesus' words at face value and see if we can translate them into our daily living.

JESUS DEMONSTRATING GREATNESS

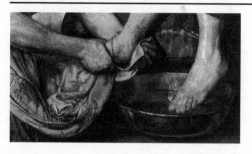

THE INCIDENT in Mark 10 is the setting for our third principle of servant leadership. It came immediately after James and John's request to sit next to Jesus when he entered his kingdom. The lesson that follows is born out of the other ten disciples' response to their fellow disciples' request. Often a leader's best opportunity to lead is when conflict arises among his followers.

THE TEN'S REACTION TO JAMES AND JOHN

The other ten disciples did not appreciate James and John's request of Jesus. Matthew and Mark said they became "indignant" with the Sons of Thunder. I believe part of their anger came from the fact that the others would have asked the same thing—if they had gotten to Jesus first! The other disciples became agitated because they shared James and John's misconception about leadership. Otherwise, they would not have been up in arms over their friends' request. If the ten other disciples had understood that leadership is not a matter of position, James and John's request would not have been a threat to them.

> IF THE TEN OTHER DISCIPLES HAD
> UNDERSTOOD THAT LEADERSHIP IS NOT A
> MATTER OF POSITION, JAMES AND JOHN'S
> REQUEST WOULD NOT HAVE BEEN
> A THREAT TO THEM.

Ambition cloaked in piety is an unhealthy mixture. The ten reacted to their friends' request like jealous siblings rather than followers of the humble Messiah. For, since following Jesus is the prerequisite to reigning with him (principle 2), the ten should have had their attention on preparing to suffer rather than on their brothers' misguided request.

JESUS' RESPONSE TO THE TEN

When the ten began their assault on James and John, Jesus must have felt more like a parent than the leader of a messianic movement. He was near the end of his earthly ministry. He must have wondered if these guys would ever get along in order to carry on the mission after his victorious death. Jesus spent much of his time disciplining and correcting his family of followers. These are responsibilities for every servant leader.

Jesus addressed his disciples as children (John 13:33). This was not a put-down. It was a term of endearment. Children are precious to parents who love them. Jesus gave those who followed him one commandment: to love one another (John 13:34). Parents continually tell their children to love each other.

Ken Hemphill, president of Southwestern Baptist Theological Seminary, has noted that leading a church as the pastor is much like being a parent in a family. Hemphill noted that Paul compared his ministry in Corinth to the role of a father when he

encouraged the Corinthians to imitate his actions (1 Cor.
4:14-21). The concept of church as family permeates the New
Testament. Hemphill advises pastors:

> Keep the biblical context of family constantly before the
> church through your preaching and teaching. But you
> must begin the process of modeling family before it will
> become reality. Start with a few key leaders and parent
> them to maturity. . . . As they grow to maturity, teach
> them to parent-disciple others. Put mature, parenting
> leaders in places of leadership in your small groups so
> that the process of parenting can be extended throughout
> the church.[1]

Parenting is a model of pastoral leadership. Leading includes
both the nurturing and discipline that parents must balance with
their children.

Parents and shepherds

Parent leader fits the biblical model of shepherd leader. The
shepherd is the biblical model for God's relationship with his
people (Ps. 23:1). It was also the designation of the Old Testament king's role among his people (2 Sam. 7:7; Zech. 11:4-17).
Jesus adopted the shepherd as his model of leadership when he
said, "I am the good shepherd. The good shepherd lays down
his life for the sheep" (John 10:11).

I want to affirm the shepherd model of leadership among
God's people. In my personal journey to discover how I should
lead, I have tried to act out every leadership style I learned
about at a conference or read about in a book. I have viewed
my role as a "rancher" to the head of a corporation. Several
years ago I stepped into the new year and announced that it
was time to move forward. We needed more space to grow.

I thought since I held the position of leader, others would follow automatically. The need was real. I was motivated. The goals seemed clear. The project fell flat on its face! There are many reasons why the project failed, but one reason was that I tried to lead in a way that was neither natural for me nor appropriate to the situation. I pushed the project rather than led the people. I acted more like a CEO with the leverage of salaries and stock options than like a shepherd who knew each sheep by name and laid down his life for them.

That failure began my discovery of these principles of servant leadership and a return to a biblical model for leadership in the church. I gave up my efforts to lead as someone told me I should lead. I began to lead as God had designed me to lead. Biblical models began to take precedence over worldly models. I am convinced that pastor as parent and pastor as shepherd are still accurate, vital models of leadership in the church. The principles inherent in both models can apply to any leadership setting.

I appreciate Lynn Anderson's work *They Smell Like Sheep*.[2] It is a balance to many church leadership models that call God's people to adopt styles based on nonbiblical patterns for leadership. Dr. Anderson has recaptured the biblical model of leader as shepherd. He reminds us that we do not have to fear the apparent dichotomy between leader and follower that this model may present. He addresses our fears when he writes:

> While some may not feel comfortable thinking of certain people as sheep and others as shepherds, our discomfort will likely disappear when we realize that the shepherding model revolves around the relationship between the shepherd and his flock. It is not a figure of strong over weak or "lords" over servants. Quite the contrary. The shepherd figure is one of love, service, and openness.[3]

Relationship is the key concept in shepherd as leader. Love, service, and openness are the characteristics of a shepherding style. Likewise, a relationship built on these characteristics works in the parent-child model. Children rebel against those with whom they have no relationship. Parishioners refuse the leadership of those who they sense do not care for them.

....

CHILDREN REBEL AGAINST THOSE WITH
WHOM THEY HAVE NO RELATIONSHIP.
PARISHIONERS REFUSE THE LEADERSHIP
OF THOSE WHO THEY SENSE
DO NOT CARE FOR THEM.

....

After Jesus corrected the thinking of James and John, he gathered his followers like a parent stopping a fight among siblings and a shepherd gathering his endangered flock. He knew that both unity of fellowship and unity of direction were necessary to carry out his mission. Jesus must have sighed as he pulled the boys together again to set their thinking and relationships straight.

THE PARADOX OF LEADING LIKE JESUS: TO BE GREAT IS TO SERVE

Leaders define what actions and attitudes will be rewarded and recognized among their followers. When followers try to define new values, the leader's responsibility is to restate the core values of the group. Businesses, organizations, and families benefit from knowing and living by their core values. In business, core values are "the organization's essential and enduring tenets—a small set of general guiding principles; not to be confused with specific cultural or operating practices; not to be compromised for financial gain or short-term expediency."[4] James Collins observes that all enduring visionary companies have a set of core values that determine the behavior of the group.

Acknowledging and living by strongly held core values can build unity and effectiveness in a church. As we began the process of enumerating our set of core values, a member of the team said, "I don't get it. Why do we need core values? We have the Bible." Good observation. I agreed that the Bible was our ultimate guide for our thinking and behavior. I said, however, that what we were looking for were *the unchanging values that made our church unique in our mission field and in the kingdom of God.* Willow Creek Community Church has helped churches understand what core values look like and the impact they can have on how a church carries out its mission.[5]

Jesus defined a core value for his leaders (then and now) when he pulled his disciples aside and taught them how to lead in the kingdom of God. He did this in response to James and John's misunderstanding of position and leadership, along with the indignant response of the other ten who shared their fellow disciples' false perception.

Jesus taught the third principle of servant leadership when he gathered his disciples to himself:

Servant leaders give up personal rights to find greatness in service to others.

How do we arrive at that principle? It is inherent in Jesus' definitions of greatness. We will see how this concept of greatness and leadership was as foreign to Jesus' followers as it is to us today. We will also see that these truths are key to understanding the mind and mission of Jesus.

Paradox is part of life and should not be feared by those who follow Jesus. Life is not—as some want it to be—simply black and white, up and down, front and back. Holograms have replaced one-dimensional drawings as models of reality. The universe is as small as it is large. We watch death give way to life, and we watch instant wealth breed poverty. We find fulfillment in suffering and emptiness in unrestrained pleasure. Children bring joy and pain to parents. Marriage is bliss and hard work. Jesus said leaders are servants. Those who lead are often bound to the goals and values of those they are leading.

Paradox is often part of a leader's style. Donald T. Phillips has recorded some of the paradoxes identifiable in President Lincoln's leadership style:

- ❖ He was charismatic yet unassuming.

- ❖ He was consistent yet flexible.

- ❖ He was the victim of vast amounts of slander and malice, yet he was also immensely popular with the troops.

- ❖ He was trusting and compassionate, yet he could also be demanding and tough.

- ❖ He was a risk taker and innovative yet patient and calculating.

- ❖ He seemed to have a revolving door of generals whom he often removed and replaced; yet, in reality, he gave them ample time and support to produce results.

- ❖ He claimed not to control events, that his policy was to have no policy, when, in actuality, he did control events to a very large degree by being aggressive, taking charge, and being extraordinarily decisive.[6]

Lincoln led as the situation demanded. While he may have appeared inconsistent at times, he modeled a style to meet the need at hand. Paradox was part of this leadership style.

Jesus exhibited paradoxical styles of leadership. He adapted his style according to those he addressed and the context of the situation:

- ❖ He was gentle as a lamb yet courageous as a lion.
- ❖ He was yielding yet aggressive when cornered by injustice.
- ❖ He was gregarious but spent much time alone.
- ❖ He was meek yet in control at all times.
- ❖ He never had a formal education, yet he taught with great authority.
- ❖ He was a conformist yet an iconoclast.
- ❖ He was a friend to the outcast yet dined with insiders.

Jesus' character never changed. He remained committed to the Father's call on his life. Out of that call and character, however, he adapted a style of leadership to meet the moment. Jesus' leadership style often presented a paradox to those who tried to follow and to those who observed him.

Jesus also used paradox in his teaching. Jesus taught, "Whoever finds his life will lose it, and whoever loses his life for my sake will find it" (Matt. 10:39). "So the last will be first, and the first will be last" (Matt. 20:16). "The kingdom of heaven is like a mustard seed" (Matt. 13:31). "Whoever humbles himself will be exalted" (Matt. 23:12). Jesus effectively wove contrasting images to introduce his message to the various people who sought him.

Paradox gives a leader the power to relay the complexities of a vision. Seemingly opposite images create a tension that is necessary if we are to find the truth. Great leaders use paradox to state the values of the new reality. Jesus defined greatness and leadership with paradox. The images confused the disciples, as it baffles some of us today. What was his picture? Jesus

painted greatness as the work of a servant. He defined leadership as the place of a slave. Both pictures seemed distorted to
those who saw them through the lenses of their culture.

HE STARTED WHERE THEY WERE

Jesus knew that his followers were trapped in the world's way
of seeing things. Part of his service to them was to lead them
into a new view of God's kingdom. He began his lesson about
leadership by noting prevailing attitudes toward greatness
and competition. The disciples did not have to look far to
find the negative and positive models of leadership Jesus
would use to teach them. Part of the power of Jesus' leadership
is that he understood and articulated the culture around him.
He chose examples from his followers' culture to help them
understand.

The power of stories

Stories often help the leader paint a picture of the future. Stories
help leaders address the issues of change. Doug Murren, author
of *Leadershift*, calls pastors to be leaders of change within the
church.[7] Murren draws from his personal experiences of leading
a church through several stages of change. He explains that effective leaders "help people experience their future before they live
it. Leaders who are able to manage paradigm shifts must learn
to make others comfortable with a vision of the future."[8]

Murren suggests that "anecdotes, folklore and metaphors"
serve to help paradigm-pioneering pastors. He believes that
"storytelling personalizes our mission and establishes memorable
patterns for the future."[9] Max DePree calls the practice "tribal
storytelling."[10] Tom Peters reminds us that "people, including
managers, do not live by pie charts alone. . . . People live, reason,
and are moved by symbols and stories."[11]

Jesus was a master at telling stories to show what the future would look like under his reign. Matthew, Jesus' first chronicler, wrote, "Jesus spoke all these things to the crowd in parables; he did not say anything to them without using a parable" (Matt. 13:34). Jesus chose stories of lost coins and sons, masters and servants, celebrations and terror, hope and loss to paint pictures of his kingdom. Jesus began where the people were. He chose pictures they understood and told stories about real people. He did this for one reason: to introduce people to the reality of what things will look like when the Son of God reigns in the hearts of people.

One day a religious leader asked Jesus what he must do to inherit eternal life. Jesus asked him if he knew what the Law said about this. He did and said, "'Love the Lord your God with all your heart and with all your soul and with all your strength and with all your mind'; and, 'Love your neighbor as yourself'" (Luke 10:27). Jesus said that the man had answered correctly. But the religious leader wanted the others to know he had a degree in Law, so he asked, "And who is my neighbor?" Jesus, undaunted and always having a story up the sleeve of his tunic, answered with the story of the Good Samaritan (Luke 10:30-37). When he finished the story and the religious leader had answered the teacher's question, everyone in the room walked away with a new definition of *neighbor*.

Jesus also used metaphors and analogies to illustrate his present and future kingdom. For example, Jesus knew that true agents of change create new containers to hold the future. He taught that the results change brings cannot be contained in old methods. "What do you do with this new reality?" people asked Jesus. "Do you stuff it into current ways of doing things? Do you build a whole new container?"

To answer the questions, Jesus used an analogy from his day to illustrate his point. He said that you cannot patch old clothes with new cloth; you cannot pour new wine into old wineskins (Matt. 9:16-17). His point? Trying to patch a tear in an old garment with new cloth only makes the tear worse when the new cloth shrinks to find its own shape. Putting new wine in well-worn, stretched containers causes them to explode. The new juices age and give off new gases that create pressure in old containers. The results of change do not belong in old containers. If you try to fill old ways with new values, both will be lost—to no one's good.

....

ANYONE WHO HAS TRIED TO MAKE
CHANGE IN A CHURCH OR BUSINESS
KNOWS THE EXPLOSION THAT CAN
OCCUR WHEN A NEW PLAN IS POURED
INTO OLD WAYS OF DOING THINGS.

....

Anyone who has tried to make change in a church or business knows the explosion that can occur when a new plan is poured into old ways of doing things. Jesus knew that change demanded new forms as well as new content. He painted an analogy from everyday life to help his followers understand the dangers of clinging to old methods when new realities come into their lives.

When I began to lead our church to a new model of doing church, I told a story using the analogy of an entrepreneur who wanted to build a new product. It went like this:

"The Product
From Warehouse to Factory: Moving the Church to Do
What It Was Commissioned to Do"

A wealthy entrepreneur, who made his money taking risks, wanted to produce a product. He did market research, studied manufacturing trends, and discovered that fiber optics was the industry of the future. Since no one would want to buy cables and switching stations, he conceived a video/voice mailbox in which one could send and receive both information and digital images. If it could be manufactured cheaply enough, every home in America would have a 2V box by the year 2000.

The entrepreneur brought his American investors together. They agreed to the project and raised sixty million dollars in less than a month. The entrepreneur hired a project manager to begin producing the product. "I want to build a video/voice mailbox. Can you do it?" asked the entrepreneur.

"Sure," said the project manager.

And he began to build the most modern, efficient, state-of-the-art warehouse.

Having provided the resources and the authority for the project, the entrepreneur left to begin another venture.

The project manager hired a staff to begin plans for a warehouse to gather all the pieces needed for the product. He traveled around the country going to seminars and other state-of-the-art warehouses so he could put together the best warehouse. He hired engineers, suppliers, and managers for the warehouse. Each month he hired more employees to code, shelf, and inventory the contents of the warehouse. He even traveled to Japan to study ware- house management, and returned with years of plans for acquiring, systematizing, and storing materials.

Halfway through the third year, when the warehouse had grown to over 100,000 square feet, 200 employees, and had an inventory of 20 million dollars, the project manager threw a company picnic. All employees, from the dockhands to the shift managers, were there with their families. They celebrated their warehouse.

Suddenly, out of the blue, a helicopter appeared over the picnic. It was the entrepreneur. His helicopter landed in the middle of the picnic, and he stepped out with a smile.

"Gentlemen," he proclaimed from a picnic stage, "I see you are celebrating. I heard about this event and came as soon as I could. I wanted to see the first video/voice mailbox you have produced. Where is it?"

The employees looked at one another, "Who is this guy? What video/voice mailbox?"

A shift manager stepped up to the entrepreneur, "Sir, you must be mistaken. This is a picnic to celebrate the most modern, efficient, state-of-the-art warehouse."

"A warehouse? I gave your project manager the authority and resources to produce a product—not build a warehouse! Where is that man?" the entrepreneur said in a big voice.

The project manager left his place at the head table and made his way to the entrepreneur. "Here I am," he said in a small voice.

"What are you doing building a warehouse? Warehouses don't produce products; they store them."

"Well, sir, I thought we could gather the goods and organize them before we built the factory and produced the product," the well-meaning project manager said.

"You thought wrong. You are fired, and I will sue you for breach of contract. I want a product, not a warehouse," said the entrepreneur.

After firing the project manager and laying off all the employees, the entrepreneur went to a group of Korean investors. "I want to build a video/voice mailbox. Can you do it?" asked the entrepreneur.

"Sure," they said.

And they began to build the most modern, efficient, state-of-the-art factory.

Jesus commissioned his people to make disciples, not warehouse Christians. Matthew 28:19 makes this very clear: "as you go, make disciples." Too many churches are warehouses of well-planned, well-managed programs for storing and shipping out believers. Jesus, on the other hand, commissioned his church to produce a product, not build warehouses.[12]

Why do I stress these parables and stories? Because authority can't accomplish much until followers understand what the leader is talking about. Jesus had the ultimate authority—and people were learning to follow him. But time and time again he had to work away at their prevailing views and guide them to the vision of the kingdom to come.

In the same way, stories, metaphors, analogies, and examples from the experiences of your followers can build a bridge from their present to your future.

WHAT THEY LEARNED IN BUSINESS SCHOOL

Jesus began his lesson on leadership with two examples from experiences common to his disciples: (1) "Lord it over them," and (2) "Exercise authority." Interestingly enough, both models are still prevalent natural styles of leading in the world.

Jesus took a jab at his culture's understanding of leadership by describing his examples as "those who are *regarded* as rulers of the Gentiles" (Mark 10:42, italics mine). Jesus made it clear that authentic rulers do not evoke these styles of leadership. Let's look closer at Jesus' two negative examples of leadership.

"Lord it over them"

The disciples knew about the "lord it over them" style of leadership. They saw it every day in their rulers, the Romans. This style is simply "might makes right"—if you have the biggest army, you run the show. I think it is called "market share" in the corporate world. We know this style very well. We daydream of opportunities to tell people what to do—with no back talk or passive-aggressive behavior. If you choose this style of leadership, the first task on your to-do list is: 1. Get a bigger army.

To lord it over someone means to subject him to your power. It implies that someone is the master and someone else is the subject. This is a very effective style of leadership—ask Hitler or Pol Pot. The concept of lord implies absolute power over another. You don't have to deal with questions or dissension. You herd people together and tell them what to do. If they disagree, you eliminate them.

> TO LORD IT OVER SOMEONE MEANS
> TO SUBJECT HIM TO YOUR POWER.
> YOU DON'T HAVE TO DEAL WITH
> QUESTIONS OR DISSENSION.

This style of leadership was common in Jesus' day too. The Romans understood how to lord it over their subjects. This is one reason they ruled the world at that time. People tend to do what they are told when they walk on a road lined with their crucified relatives. Even today governments and organizations know how to subject people to their power. Little has changed in the hearts of people since Jesus walked the earth.

Jesus used lording it over others as a negative model of leadership. On the other hand, he presented himself as "Lord" over his disciples. How did that fit with his negative example of leadership?

Jesus knew that lordship without compassion breeds abuse. Arrogance and power foster tyranny. Jesus could wear the title of Lord because of who he was as the Son of God and because no other title could describe his relationship with those who followed him.

Jesus warned against trying to lord it over others; yet, as Lord, Jesus used his power to demand absolute allegiance of his followers. Matthew 10 is a manual of discipleship. Jesus spelled out what it meant to be one of his followers. He commanded, "Anyone who loves his father or mother more than me is not worthy of me; anyone who loves his son or daughter more than me is not worthy of me; and anyone who does not take his cross and follow me is not worthy of me" (Matt. 10:37-38).

We need to remember that, as true Lord, Jesus could make these claims on his followers. The problem with human leaders is that we are not Jesus; therefore, any attempt to be lord will result in our ultimate destruction and the ruin of others.

Jesus held up a popular model of leadership for his disciples. He wanted them to know that this was a choice they could make when leading others. Their selfish nature and their culture's acceptance of this model made it a potential option of leadership. Jesus, however, desired his followers to lead another way.

"Exercise authority"

Jesus' other negative leadership model involved those he called "their high officials." We get our English prefix *mega-* from the Greek word Jesus used to describe these leaders. This leadership style involves using the authority of your position to make things happen. This concept fits James and John's request of Jesus. They thought that if they could get the position, they could exercise authority over others. They wanted to be megadisciples!

Authority is a leader's vehicle of power. It gives him the ability to move others to action. If you choose this style of leadership, the first item on your to-do list is: 1. Get a bigger office. James

MacGregor Burns notes, however, "All leaders are actual or potential power holders, but not all power holders are leaders."[13]

························

YOU MAY FIND YOURSELF IN A POSITION OF LEADERSHIP, YET YOU CANNOT SEEM TO GET PEOPLE TO FOLLOW YOU.

························

You may find yourself in a position of leadership, yet you cannot seem to get people to follow you. One of two problems may exist. Either you haven't gone to the seminar on "how to use your positional authority to get people to work for you" (hard to fit on the front of a brochure), or you have not studied Jesus' source of authority. Richard Foster concludes that "the spiritual authority of Jesus is an authority not found in a position or a title, but in a towel."[14]

Jesus understood authority. He knew leaders could misuse their authority to make innocent people do what they wanted them to do. During the last week of his earthly ministry, Jesus attacked the misuse of authority by the religious leaders of his day. He told the people to do what their leaders taught them to do because the leaders held positions of authority given by God. On the other hand, Jesus told the people not to do what their leaders did because "they do not practice what they preach" (Matt. 23:3). Jesus recognized the authority of the religious leaders (even though they did not recognize his authority) while pointing out their misuse of it. We will see in principle 6 of servant leadership that shared authority is essential to a leader's success.

Jesus used his authority to teach his design for discipleship. Matthew 5–7 is the heart of Jesus' teaching on how life would look if he reigned in people's hearts. He raised the Old Covenant laws to new heights of expectations. Yet he offered the blessedness of an impoverished spirit. When he had concluded his teaching, Matthew wrote, "the crowds were amazed at his teaching, because he taught as one who had authority, and not as their teachers of the law" (Matt. 7:28-29).

Jesus used his positional authority as leader to accomplish his mission. He used these aspects of leadership to guide his followers toward his vision of the kingdom of God. So in a sense, Jesus was able to be Lord in the way that earthly leaders could only attempt to lord it over others. Jesus cautioned against these two natural methods of leading because he knew people's hearts and how easily such authority could be abused.

WHAT STYLE OF GREATNESS DO YOU SEEK?

WE CAN study Jesus' definition of greatness. But it becomes difficult to apply in an atmosphere of the world's competition. How do we become great in the way Jesus taught?

A MOVE AWAY FROM THESE
NEGATIVE LEADERSHIP STYLES

Currently there is a trend away from the two negative styles of leadership that Jesus described to his disciples. The trend is toward service in the marketplace. This is not self-serving customer service to ensure greater bottom lines, but it is a call from self-interest to service. Peter Block, the author of *Stewardship*,[15] calls for heads of organizations and companies to see themselves as stewards. Block asks leaders to have the goal of stewardship, not leadership.

> Stewardship asks us to serve our organizations and be accountable to them without caretaking and without

taking control. And in letting caretaking and control go, we hold on to the spiritual meaning of stewardship: to honor what has been given us, to use power with a sense of grace, and to pursue purposes that transcend short-term self-interest.[16]

Stewardship is about governance of an organization, according to Block. It is about holding something in trust for another. It is "giving order to the dispersion of power."[17] Stewards choose partnership over patriarchy, empowerment over dependency, and service over self-interest. Service, Block argues, comes when a person commits to something outside herself. Block has captured the sense of service as an essential ingredient in the leading process.

Max DePree asks us to look at leadership as service and the leader as a steward:

> Try to think about a leader, in the words of the gospel writer Luke, as "one who serves." Leadership is a concept of owing certain things to the institution. It is a way of thinking about institutional heirs, a way of thinking about stewardship as contrasted with ownership. . . . The art of leadership requires us to think about the leader-as-steward in terms of relationships: of assets and legacy, of momentum and effectiveness, of civility and values.[18]

DePree teaches that the leader owes the institution certain assets like financial health and a legacy of empowered people. Leaders are obligated to give momentum through a clear vision. Effectiveness comes from "enabling others to reach their potential—both their personal potential and their corporate or institutional potential."[19] Leaders owe those who follow the civility of "identifying values" that give meaning to their work. Leading,

writes DePree, is the "opportunity to make a meaningful difference in the lives of those who permit leaders to lead."[20]

These current trends away from "lord it over" and "exercise
authority" are healthy ones. They provide a starting point for
people to consider Jesus' teachings about leadership. The acceptance of books like *Jesus, CEO*[21] signal that Jesus is still a source
of wisdom in the marketplace. As a follower of Jesus, you have
the opportunity to build a bridge from contemporary leadership
situations to the teachings of Jesus. The use of Jesus' stories,
metaphors, and analogies is an excellent way to introduce God's
truth into a conversation or board meeting.

"NOT SO WITH YOU!"

Jesus abruptly turned his lesson away from contemporary thinking to kingdom priorities when he said, "Not so with you"
(Mark 10:43). This statement is a sign of God's presence. Following Jesus means that the rules have changed. The landscape is
different. The road ends on another horizon. "Not so with you"
declares that the kingdom of heaven is at hand. Those who follow Jesus must recognize that conventional wisdom and power
methods are not the best way to lead among God's people.

....

JESUS MADE A DISTINCTION BETWEEN
HOW THE WORLD LEADS AND HOW
HIS FOLLOWERS ARE TO LEAD
AMONG THEMSELVES.

....

By saying, "Not so with you," Jesus made a distinction
between how the world leads and how his followers are to lead
among themselves. *Please remember that what Jesus teaches about
greatness and leadership cannot be expected of leaders who do not*

embrace Jesus as their final authority. Naturally, without the presence of Jesus' Spirit and the values of his kingdom in our lives, we cannot accept the definitions nor the actions his words imply. Without the Spirit of Jesus in our hearts and minds, we will gravitate to natural ways of becoming great and getting to the front of the line. Those outside a relationship with Christ may appreciate the wisdom of Jesus, but they cannot live out his teachings fully. A heart in relationship with the Teacher is necessary before you can know the meaning of greatness and leadership in the kingdom of God.

YOU KNOW YOU'RE A SERVANT WHEN . . .

Jesus modeled greatness through service to others when he did not seek a public office, earn a degree, lead an army, or discover some scientific truth. Jesus' entire ministry was about service to his Father in heaven, service to his mission, service to his followers, and, ultimately, service to those he came to save. Jesus was a great man because he was a servant. We acknowledge him as great because he lived beyond the noise of life and purposefully lived to bring people closer to their Creator. As Lord of all, he might have lived above us and demanded blind allegiance. But he served us, teaching us the truth and how to live by it. He served us in our misunderstanding, our selfishness, and our weakness. He saw what we needed and helped us. He knew where we needed to be and took us there—with great love and respect for us.

We have lost this fundamental model of greatness in our personality-centered culture. Greatness seems to belong to the builders and those of influence. Greatness is equated with name recognition and social status. Churches and nonprofit organizations have become too much like the world in this respect. We hand out certificates of greatness to those who grow the biggest organization or gather the most people on a weekend. We honor those who sit in places of power. We have forgotten that greatness among God's people begins with service, and service implies labor without accolades.

....

WE HAND OUT CERTIFICATES OF
GREATNESS TO THOSE WHO GROW THE
BIGGEST ORGANIZATION OR GATHER THE
MOST PEOPLE ON A WEEKEND.

....

I led a church leadership conference a year or two ago in a southern state. When I came into the place where the meal was served, I noticed two tables with the sign: "Reserved for Servers." Both tables were empty, while the other tables were full. People were even looking for places to sit because all the other places were filled. When I got up to speak, I wondered out loud if it was their respect for the "reserved" sign or their fear of being known as "servers" that kept people from sitting at those tables! We too often forget to equate greatness with service. I told the group that under Jesus' model of leadership, one of those "Reserved for Servers" signs should have been on every table.

Being a servant is not one of our natural goals. After the deaths of Princess Diana and Mother Teresa, a friend asked me, "Who would you rather have been?" He knew I would have to choose between what I thought I ought to say and what I wanted to say. Given the choice, most of us would rather be the prince or princess of Wales than a servant to orphans in India. I said that I would rather have been Mother Teresa and explained that her life modeled more of how Jesus lived his life than Diana's did. I must admit that I have wondered what it would be like to be treated like royalty. My human desire to be known as great sometimes outweighs my call to be a servant in the streets of my city.

The test of whether or not you have accepted Jesus' teaching about greatness is how you react when others treat you like a servant. One of my staff members attended a Bill Gothard seminar several years ago. Once you go to one of his meetings, you receive a birthday card from him for the rest of your life. I think you can move seven times without ever leaving a forwarding address and still count on your birthday card from Bill! One day, the staff member came into my office and showed me the birthday card he had received from the Gothard organization. It read, "The true test of a servant is if I act like one when I am treated like one." He had teased before that we all like to be referred to as servants of God until we are treated like servants. The reality is that if you seek to find greatness in service to your peers, you can count on being treated like a servant.

BEING FIRST IN LINE

Jesus then said, "If you want to be first." This phrase implies leadership. We get our English prefix *proto-* from the Greek word for *first.* It means first in a line or series. Leaders are first in line. They are out front defining reality, painting the future, and showing the way to it. Leaders are first in line for a new type of reality.

Robert Greenleaf recognized two concepts of being the leader. One is being the lone chief on top of a hierarchical structure.[22] The other is being the principal leader as *primus inter pares*—"first among equals."[23] He notes that in this latter model there is still a "first," but that leader is not the chief. Greenleaf concludes, "The difference may appear to be subtle, but it is important that the primus constantly test and prove that leadership among a group of able peers." Greenleaf's "first among equals" is another way of being first as Jesus taught his followers.

The constant test and proof of being the primus under Jesus' definition is how you serve the others.

Jesus created an apparent absurdity when he said, "Whoever wants to be first in line must become a slave." The disciples understood "first in line." They scratched their heads over becoming a slave. Slave in this verse was a *doulos* slave. In the first century, this human being was the lowest rung of the social ladder. These people were bought and sold as property. A *doulos* slave had no rights or privileges, no wants or desires, only the commands of the master. The disciples, as Jews, refused to be slaves to anyone. That was what the Exodus was about. They rejected Jesus' picture of leadership initially because it was too strange to put the pieces together. How could you be first in line by becoming someone on the lowest rung of the ladder?

Being a slave involves several things: the loss of property, separation from roots, abuse by unkind owners, loss of individuality, and, of course, no freedom to choose. Being a slave means giving up personal rights. This is the first step to being first among God's people. Why? You cannot be a servant until you give up your personal rights to be served. Greatness in service to others can never occur as long as you insist that it is your right that others serve you.

What advantage is there to giving up your right to be served? How does that act enhance your ability to be a servant leader? Richard Foster helps us see that giving up our right to be served actually leads to freedom.

> When we choose to be a servant, we give up the right to be in charge. There is great freedom in this. If we voluntarily choose to be taken advantage of, then we cannot be manipulated. When we choose to be a servant, we surrender the right to decide who and when we will serve. We become available and vulnerable.[24]

Giving up our right to be served frees us to serve others. Choosing the place and work of a slave removes every barrier that keeps people apart.

....

WE LIVE IN A CULTURE WHERE THE INDIVIDUAL HAS BEEN MOVED TO THE CENTER OF THE UNIVERSE.

....

We live in a culture where the individual has been moved to the center of the universe. When that takes place, the rights of the individual reign over the needs of others. Until rights are relinquished, service is less likely to happen. Service can occur, but it will be self-serving rather than others oriented. Learning to serve begins with following the Master. Becoming a slave to God is how we become "first" among our peers. Being a slave is not part of our natural feelings. How can we understand this principle?

Wellington Boone, the author of *Breaking Through* and a popular speaker in the Promise Keeper's movement, has put a unique twist on what it means to be an African-American and speak of becoming a slave of Christ.[25] He writes that blacks in this country have a two-hundred-year advantage over others in learning to be slaves of Christ and servants to others! He writes, "Blacks have had more than two centuries of training in being a slave of man. It can be added as long-term qualification to prepare them to be a fine slave of God or to rule as a king."[26]

I agree with Rev. Boone that being a "slave to God" (Rom. 6:19-23) is a biblical model for a Christian's lifestyle. I would add that the model of slavery as a pattern for discipleship among white Americans may be even more difficult to comprehend. Why? Whites have been the owners! Moving from owner and master to slave may be more difficult than returning to a previous historical era to comprehend the teachings of Jesus. This model for following Christ is a primary reason it is so hard for postmodern people to risk true discipleship.[27]

Finding greatness in service begins by giving up your personal right to be served. This principle of servant leadership may be the most difficult to comprehend today. We have so few contemporary models to observe and follow. Centuries separate us from the context of Jesus' teaching. How can this principle become part of your leadership style?

HOW CAN I LEAD THIS WAY?

What does this picture of leadership look like in real life? How can servants and slaves really lead? The answer poses a real dilemma for a disciple of Jesus. How do you take what you learned in business school and join it to the sayings of Jesus? Is that possible? Is there another way?

Servants and slaves do not define leadership in the world's dictionary. Many people understand the idea of being a servant and forfeiting personal rights as self-effacing. I remember when my wife, who was a public-school teacher at the time, was confronted by a school counselor. My wife had confessed her faith in Jesus. The counselor said that she didn't like Christians because they caused such a low self-esteem in others. The counselor equated confessing that you are a sinner with having a low self-esteem. She would no doubt have felt that seeing yourself as a servant meant not having a "healthy" self-image too.

Jesus came to show what life in the kingdom of God looked like, not to modify how the world did things. The ways of God work in the hallways of humanity only when Jesus reigns in people's hearts. Any follower of Christ who seeks to lead as Jesus led must be willing to be treated like Jesus. Some will follow. Others will throw stones.

....

JESUS CAME TO SHOW WHAT LIFE IN THE
KINGDOM OF GOD LOOKED LIKE, NOT TO
MODIFY HOW THE WORLD DID THINGS.

....

By his own example

Jesus lived the answer to the question of how to lead like a servant.
He concluded his lesson on greatness by saying, "For even the Son
of Man did not come to be served, but to serve, and to give his life
as a ransom for many" (Mark 10:45). Jesus stated his mission with
those words. He knew his disciples would not get it until he completed his mission. He had to say, in essence, "Watch me. I will
show you how this works. I have not come to be served by you,
I have come to serve you. I will also give my life as a payment so
that many will be freed to a relationship with God." Jesus knew he
had to model this lesson before his students would ever be able to
live it out.

Jesus was not a teacher who only defined his terms; he also
modeled what he called others to do. James, John, and the other
ten disciples experienced what Jesus taught as they followed him
to his death, burial, and resurrection. They soon saw that servant
leadership meant ultimately giving up their lives so others could
have the life God desired for them.

This kind of service is the basis for servant leadership in the
home. Marriage is in many ways giving up personal rights to find
greatness in service to another. The traditional vows of marriage,
which continue to be the ones chosen by the vast majority of
couples I marry, imply service to the partner no matter the circumstances. Marriage works when you come to the place where
the other's well-being is as important as your own.

I realize that some counselors could argue that giving up personal rights can be dangerous to an individual's self-image and,
therefore, can create an unhealthy marriage. And I admit that I

have seen marriages where a husband sees his wife as a servant and she does not know how to protect her personal boundaries. On the other hand, the nature of love is to lay down willingly what is rightfully yours in order to serve the needs of another person. Marriage can be healthy when both partners find greatness in service rather than in being served.

Sacrificial service is certainly part of parenting. I once co-led a Jesus on Leadership group with our Women's Ministry Team leader. The group was made up of women who led different areas of ministry to women in our church and community. When we came to the principle about giving up your personal rights and finding greatness in service to others, I commented that this was a difficult concept for many men. I wondered how they felt about it. They began to laugh. I asked, "What's so funny?" One woman spoke for the group when she said, "Look, when you're a mother, you gave up your personal rights to find greatness in service the day you had your first child!" I laughed too. Parenting is giving up your personal rights and finding greatness in service to your children. I guess most mothers learn that principle sooner than fathers.

In the same way, a father can live out this principle when he chooses to modify his career goals in order to serve the mission of his family above the goals of a company. This does not mean living your life out through your children. It does not mean setting aside providing in the best way you can for your family. It does mean, however, that you serve the young person growing under your care in order for her to live out God's plan for her life. Modeling greatness in service is one way to teach your children this principle.

The one true model

Jesus deserves service from those he created! He, however, came to serve. He came to give his life as a payment for the sins of others. Jesus came to give his life as a ransom so creation could be set free from its separation from its Creator. A ransom in the ancient world was a payment to free a slave or prisoner.[28] As the Son of Man, Jesus saw his life as one of sacrifice so that others could benefit.

I believe Jesus is our only true model of servant leadership. He served others by giving his life for them. His entire life mission was to free others, not to gain position for himself. This is a mystery to the world, but it is the heart of servant leadership after the teachings of Jesus. Anyone who seeks to lead in the body of Christ must submit himself to the lordship of Jesus in his life. Only then can one begin to understand why servants are great and slaves are first.

FOR STUDY AND REFLECTION

- What were your first impressions when you read Jesus' teaching on leadership to his disciples? Did you accept it at face value? If so, have you discarded it or embraced it? If not, how have you explained its clear message?

- Complete the statement, "I am like the ten disciples because . . ." Your answer may be like mine, "I am naturally competitive and want to be up front. It irks me when someone else reaches the finish line before I do."

- Make a list of five ways you can lead by taking the place of a slave in the marketplace, in your home, and in your church.

- One of Jesus' core values for leadership can be summarized as "Greatness is defined by service" and "Leaders serve others first." What are the core values for your leadership roles?

Endnotes for Principle #3

1. Ken Hemphill, *The Antioch Effect* (Nashville: Broadman & Holman, 1994), 112.

2. Lynn Anderson, *They Smell Like Sheep* (West Monroe, La.: Howard, 1997).

3. Ibid., 19.

4. James C. Collins and Jerry I. Porras, *Built to Last* (New York: Harper Business, 1997), 73.

5. Lynne and Bill Hybels, *Rediscovering Church* (Grand Rapids: Zondervan, 1995), 183–94.

6. Donald T. Phillips, *Lincoln on Leadership* (New York: Warner Books, 1993), 79–80.

7. Doug Murren, *Leadershift* (Ventura, Calif.: Regal, 1994).

8. Ibid., 151.

9. Ibid., 154.

10. Max DePree, *Leadership Is an Art* (New York: Doubleday, 1989), 72.

11. Tom Peters, *Thriving on Chaos,* Perennial Library Ed. (New York: Harper & Row, Perennial Library Edition, 1987), 506.

12. The principles of this story have been published in *Growing Churches* (April, May, June 1993) "From Warehouses to Factories" (also published in Ministry Advantage, a newsletter of Fuller Seminary, Pasadena, Calif.). If I were telling the story today, I would title it "From Mainframe to Local Area Network: Moving the church from being single server to customized service." The next generation would understand "From a LAN to the Internet: Moving the church from local area mentality to being a world-wide influence."

13. James MacGregor Burns, *Leadership* (New York: Harper & Row, 1978), 18.

14. Richard J. Foster, *Celebration of Discipline* (New York: HarperCollins, 1988), 128.

15. Peter Block, *Stewardship, Choosing Service over Self-Interest* (San Francisco: Berrett-Koehler, 1993).

16. Ibid., 22.

17. Ibid., 18.

18. DePree, *Leadership Is an Art,* 10.

19. Ibid., 16.

20. Ibid., 19.

21. Laurie Beth Jones, *Jesus, CEO* (New York: Hyperion, 1995).

22. Robert K. Greenleaf, *Servant Leadership* (Mahwah, N.J.: Paulist, 1977), 61.

23. Ibid.

24. Foster, *Celebration of Discipline,* 132.

25. Wellington Boone, *Breaking Through* (Nashville: Broadman & Holman, 1995).

26. Ibid., 77.

27. Popular books like James Redfield's *The Celestine Prophecy* (New York: Warner, 1993) spell out the self-becoming-god pattern of thinking among many Western minds. Without a reference to God or an awareness of God's work

in a person's life, the choice of "vibrating to a higher realm of existence" or becoming a "slave to God" seems an obvious one.

28. William F. Arndt and F. Wilbur Gingrich, *A Greek-English Lexicon of the New Testament & Other Early Christian Literature* (Chicago: The University of Chicago Press, 1957), 483.

TAKE RISKS

VICTORY is only wrested by running risks.
WINSTON CHURCHILL *Churchill on Leadership*

IT IS still a great risk in our society
to offer new rules for the game.
JOEL A. BARKER *Future Edge*

PARADIGM pioneers are always inquisitive, humble
students. If they assume the status of expert, they
can be the church's greatest obstacle to growth.
DOUG MURREN *Leadershift*

BY AVOIDING risk we really risk what's most important
in life—reaching toward growth, our potential,
and a true contribution to a common good.
MAX DEPREE *Leading without Power*

I RECENTLY interviewed a prospective staff member. At one point, the candidate turned the questioning to the interviewers. "Would you consider your church willing to take risks?" Silence. No one had ever asked us that question before. I held my tongue—and my breath. I had learned that interviewing potential staff and church members was a way to get a fresh read on our church.

As individuals began to speak, I was pleased to hear our search team say that we were willing to take risks. Each one had an experience in which he or she believed our church had risked something—or, at least, had refused the status quo—to accomplish our mission to make disciples. One of the members did say we did not take "the wild-haired kind" of risks. After each person had spoken, it seemed to me that we perceived ourselves to be moderate risk takers. That's the way I, too, saw our church. As the leader, of course, I wanted to hear each person say we'd do anything to carry out our mission, but we were not there yet. We agreed that we took enough risks to stay on mission, but we were not known for our bungee jumping.

The candidate then asked, "What is the greatest risk you have taken personally?" I did not hold my tongue on that one. I told him and the group that my greatest personal risk was staying on the course we had begun to chart five years earlier. My greatest risk did not come in the form of building three buildings and acquiring more land or changing our worship style or addressing some moral issue in a Sunday morning message. I had faced my greatest risk at this church when I'd had to decide if I would indeed carry out the mission and vision I believed God wanted our church to live out. That decision had risked my comfort, future, and place of acceptance among my peers. Deciding to lead the church to carry out its mission without compromise was the biggest risk I had taken up to that point in my life.

Those two questions, I believe, are diagnostic questions for any church and/or church leader. "Do you consider yourselves risk takers?" and "What is the greatest personal risk you have taken?" reveal in a church and its leaders the desire (or lack of desire) to move ahead and risk everything for its mission. Refusal to take those risks prevents a leader from moving toward the goal.

JESUS, THE GREAT RISK TAKER

NEXT to his death on the cross, washing the feet of his disciples was Jesus' ultimate model of servant leadership. On his last night with his leadership team, Jesus chose to serve those who should have served him. Many of us don't immediately see what kind of risk that was. Jesus was giving up his place at the head of the table. This is just the kind of risk he will require of us. But before we try to apply this to ourselves, we need to understand how Jesus could do what he did.

What was the source of Jesus' willingness to risk his place at the head table to serve his followers? Where did Jesus find enough confidence to give himself such a glaring demotion? What can his actions and motives show us?

. . . .

NEXT TO HIS DEATH ON THE CROSS,
WASHING THE FEET OF HIS DISCIPLES
WAS JESUS' ULTIMATE MODEL
OF SERVANT LEADERSHIP.

. . . .

Every great leader takes risks—taking others to places no one has gone before. Since a leader sets the pace for his group, he is free to go out of the ordinary and to ask startling questions. But when a leader guides people to new places, he often risks his position, power, and provisions. After all, what if others in an organization aren't feeling so adventurous? What if a follower worries about money a lot? What if the mission agency "doesn't get it" when the leader is taking Christ's followers into uncharted territory? What if the people with the purse strings have a different definition of success than the leader has? We can begin to imagine all kinds of situations in which good leadership equals risk taking, which could well equal losses. Kouzes and Posner describe leaders this way:

> Leaders are pioneers—people who are willing to step out into the unknown. They are people who are willing to take risks, to innovate and experiment in order to find new and better ways of doing things.[1]

Leaders take risks because they see the future before anyone else can. This ability places leaders on the horizon rather than in the comfort of a settler's home.

Joel Barker compares pioneering leaders to settlers:

> What's the difference between a pioneer and a settler?
> It is the settler who always is calling toward the horizon, "Is it safe out there now?" The voice calling back, "Of course it's safe out here!" is the pioneer's. That is because the pioneers take the risk, go out early, and make the new territory safe.[2]

Winston Churchill was known as a man who took huge risks. Steven Hayward has observed, "Churchill's refusal throughout his career to practice bland, risk-averse politics stands out as his most striking leadership attribute. Churchill's audacious and risk-taking character was at the core of his genius."[3] Hayward also noted that his risk taking "also constituted the chief liability of his long career and nearly led to his ruin." But Churchill overcame that liability by learning from his mistakes. Great leaders take risks.

Max DePree reminds us that "by avoiding risk we really risk what's most important in life—reaching toward growth, our potential, and a true contribution to a common goal."[4] DePree says it takes a special kind of risk to join an organization purely to serve. "Wherever or however we serve," he concludes, "we can't avoid the central conundrum of risk: to risk nothing is perhaps the greatest risk of all."

Standing on the edge

A leader is a pioneer because she goes to the edge of a current reality and takes the next step. Upon seeing the new reality, she invites others to join her on the edge. Not everyone is drawn to the edge, but most people admire those who stand on it.

Doug Murren reminds us that the great leaders in the Bible—Moses, Joshua, Jesus, Peter, and Paul—were all paradigm pioneers. "All paradigm pioneers have a different spirit from the naysayers about them. They have the ability to see a new thing, to perceive a bright future, to tap into the power of God."[5]

—By the power of God

What distinguishes leaders under Christ's lordship from those who merely lead by their natural abilities? The difference is simple: Christ's servants tap into God's power. Otherwise, how could they see the future and have the courage to pioneer their way into it? God's power enables them to see the vision and help others toward it. How does a person—leader or otherwise—gain access to such power? Through faith, of course. After all, faith is the confidence in things promised by God—but often not yet seen by others.

> CHRIST'S SERVANTS TAP INTO GOD'S
> POWER. OTHERWISE, HOW COULD THEY
> SEE THE FUTURE AND HAVE THE COURAGE
> TO PIONEER THEIR WAY INTO IT?

Hebrews 11:1 defines faith as being "certain of what we do not see." The people described in that chapter are heroes of faith (servant leaders, I would call them) because they trusted God at his word and "saw" what God promised them. Although Abraham could not see the Promised Land, he trusted God enough to pack up his camels and leave home. He became the "Father of Faith" and leader of God's people because he trusted God enough to step out on the edge. What was the source of his ability to risk? His trust in the God who called him to follow. It becomes clear that God's people have the capacity to be visionaries, pioneers—leaders. With faith, we see God's reality. And since we see it and are confident of it, we are able to go there and take others with us.

If taking risks is inherently part of leadership, what does Jesus teach us about the unique nature of risk taking?

John's Gospel is a reflection on the life of Jesus. The elder apostle chose seven sayings and seven signs of Jesus to give his readers an opportunity to trust that Jesus was the Son of God (John 20:30-31). John is the only Gospel writer to tell about Jesus' washing his disciples' feet. This act was prophetic. It was as important as equating himself with the bread and wine of the Passover meal—and it involved a purpose we will explore in the next chapter.

Leading from power

We commonly visualize a leader standing before his troops on the eve of battle, making the speech of a lifetime. We see President Roosevelt standing before congress declaring war on Japan. We envision President Kennedy prophesying that we would put a man on the moon by the end of the decade. We see President Bush unleashing the nation's military power during Desert Storm. We expect leaders to lead from positions of power. We want them to stand before their people and call upon the best in them to carry the torch on the next leg of the journey.

Leaders often elevate themselves to places bigger than life to inspire their people. I remember seeing Bill Gates on television at the launching of Windows 95. His ubiquitous presence and trinitronic imaging called the world of software users to join him as he led into the future. Who wouldn't want to sell and service a product for a guy that appeared bigger than life simultaneously all over the world? Bigger-than-life helps when leading.

These grand corporate images have influenced Christ's church. Sometimes church leaders look for that powerful position to fuel their leadership. Sometimes we begin to believe that weakness could never be part of the image of the "man of God."

Is that where you are now? Are you putting too much confidence in your position? Possibly your greatest risk at this time would be to give up that place of power. Move into the ranks of the followers. Christ could command the allegiance of his disciples because of who he was. They admired the power he demonstrated over demons, diseases, and the elements. But they stayed with the Lord Jesus because he loved them. He served them. And he took them to places they would never go on their own.

Three facts he led by

On his last night with his closest followers, Jesus declared himself the fulfillment of the ancient Passover meal. This meal symbolized how God delivered his people from slavery. By his actions on that night, Jesus announced that his death was the final exodus of God for his people. No longer would people be enslaved to sin and death. During this prophetic meal, Jesus risked his place of leadership among his followers when he left his place at the table.

Why would he lower himself to slave status when he only had one night left on earth with his followers? Where did the vision and confidence to take such a risk come from? The answer is in the Bible. In verse 3 of John 13, it says: "Jesus knew that the Father had put all things under his power, and that he had come from God and was returning to God; so he got up." Jesus trusted that his Father was in complete control of his life. What did he have to lose by leaving the table to serve those who followed him? The three facts John records for us are the basis of Jesus' confidence.

JESUS KNEW THAT GOD "HAD PUT ALL THINGS UNDER HIS POWER." He knew that God was in control of his life and ministry. He had come to do the will of his Father. By the time of the meal, Jesus knew God's call on his life as the Sent One from God. Jesus had settled this during his temptation. God had confirmed it at his transfiguration. Jesus knew that because God had gifted him with his mission and the abilities to carry it out, he didn't have to worry about losing anything of importance. Everything came from the Father. All power came from the Father.

JESUS KNEW "HE HAD COME FROM GOD." Jesus knew that his Father in heaven was the source of his mission in life. John's Gospel also tells us, "In the beginning was the Word, and the Word was with God, and the Word was God" (John 1:1). We have read Philippians 2:5-7, which declared the preexistence of Christ and his willingness to empty himself into the form of a human. Jesus was confident he had come from God. This led to his confidence that what he was doing was part of his heavenly Father's ultimate plan for his life.

Jesus Trusted That He "Was Returning to God." Jesus trusted that his life would not end in death. He told his disciples, "In my Father's house are many rooms; if it were not so, I would have told you. I am going there to prepare a place for you. And if I go and prepare a place for you, I will come back and take you to be with me that you also may be where I am" (John 14:2-3). He knew that he would return to his eternal place as God in heaven.

....

WHEN WE TRUST THAT GOD IS IN CONTROL OF OUR LIFE, WE CAN TAKE BIG RISKS.

....

Jesus' trust in these three realities made it possible for Jesus to "demote" himself willingly and without fear. He knew who he was; he knew whose he was, and he knew where he was going. When we are sure of these three truths, we have nothing to fear. Our position with God is forever secure—as we are obedient to his will and purpose. John wrote that it was because Jesus trusted in these realities, along with the certainty of divine timing and his love for his followers, that he got up from the Passover table, got dressed like a servant, and did the work of a slave.

This insight into the source of Jesus' confidence to risk service forms the foundation for our fourth principle of servant leadership:

Servant leaders can risk serving others when they trust that God is in control of their lives.

When we trust that God is in control of our life, we can take big risks. We can relinquish impressive positions. We can act like true servants without being insecure or defensive. A servant leader can risk her place of leadership for the purpose of service. A servant leader trusts that in her relationship with Christ, God has placed all power under her, that she has come from God, and that she is returning to God.

HOW YOU CAN
TAKE THE RISK

YOU may be asking, "How am I supposed to find that kind of confidence and trust? Those realities are not true in my life!" You can have the same confidence Jesus had—by learning to truly trust God with your life.

These three realities help us get over the fear that we will lose something we've gained for ourselves if we leave our place at the head table. We tend to believe the myth that it is our effort alone that gets us what we have: "Breaks come to those who make them." A person of faith, on the other hand, admits that anything good that happens in life is from Jesus. Once we have allowed God to develop a humble heart in us, we can see that life is a gift and "every good and perfect gift is from above" (James 1:17).

We won't be so nervous to protect what we have when we truly believe that we have very little to do with who we are and what we have. This reality supports what we learned about waiting on God to exalt us. You did not earn your place at the head table. God chose you for that place. Your fear to risk that place for the mission of God points to your lack of trust in the God who got you there.

Now, I need to stress that if you have found leadership because you sought it on your own, you had better get very good at protecting your position. *Places earned by self-effort alone are places that can be taken by someone else's greater self-effort.* Leadership among God's people does not rely solely on self-effort.

....

PLACES EARNED BY SELF-EFFORT ALONE ARE PLACES THAT CAN BE TAKEN BY SOMEONE ELSE'S GREATER SELF-EFFORT.

....

ALL THINGS ARE UNDER YOUR POWER

The first phrase that describes Jesus in John 13:3 is that he "knew that the Father had put all things under his power." You say, "OK, I know that about Jesus. How can I know that about me?" First a word of caution. A phrase like "all things are under your power" can be misleading in a culture that has elevated self to god status. I am not saying that this reality is inherent in who you are naturally. Such a reality can only come in a personal relationship with God through Jesus Christ.

Many things happen when you give your life to Christ. For one thing, your status with God changes. You move from slave status to child status. You become a child of God and a coheir with Christ (Rom. 8:16-17). "In Christ" refers to your relationship of trust in Jesus as your Savior and Lord. Paul took time to explain what a life in Christ looks like. Paul wrote that after Jesus' resurrection, God seated his Son "at his right hand in the heavenly realms, far above all rule and authority, power and dominion. . . . And God placed all things under his feet" (Eph. 1:20-22). Then Paul wrote that, on the basis of our relationship with God through Christ, "God raised us up with Christ and seated us with him in the heavenly realms" (Eph. 2:6). We can conclude that through our relationship with Christ we can trust "that the Father . . . put all things under his power."

How does this translate into your life as a servant leader? It means you can trust that God has provided everything you need to carry out his mission through your life. God has empowered you with the Holy Spirit, the authority of the name of Jesus, and the assurance that all your needs will be met. When you really trust that God has done these things, risking your place at the head table to do the mission of God is no risk at all. Risking service to those entrusted to you on the mission is part of the confidence you find in knowing God.

How does this work in the workplace?

This characteristic of a servant leader equals confidence in the workplace. Coworkers and those over you should observe a willingness in you to risk your place at the corporate head table because of your confidence that God is in control of your life. Those who work with you should observe your faith along with your talents and training. Taking risks within the guidelines handed to you can be an opportunity to share your ultimate status as a child of the King. Even in the face of failure, you can share the reality of God's presence in your life and the confidence that gives you to be the kind of worker your company appreciates.

The story of Daniel is an example of this principle. Chosen for fast-track training in service to the king, Daniel and his four friends were given a chance to overcome the cruel circumstances of being captives in a foreign land. Daniel trusted that his service to God was more important than his service to any earthly king—even if it jeopardized his chances for advancement. He risked his place at the head table when he refused to accept the king's training table in favor of foods chosen by God. Daniel appropriately challenged the status quo of Babylon by asking the official to test the ways of God against the ways of the world. After just ten days, Daniel and his friends "looked healthier and better nourished than any of the young men who ate the royal food" (Dan. 1:15). Daniel's trust in God—even down to laws about what to eat and drink—gave him confidence to risk his place at the king's table. In the long run, this confidence in God became the very reason the king chose Daniel to rule with him.

YOU CAME FROM GOD

Jesus came from God. John 1:1-18 describes this truth. Every follower of Christ trusts that life comes from God. Scripture makes it clear that all life is sacred because its source is God. Jeremiah declared his trust that God had called him to mission before he formed him in his mother's womb (Jer. 1:5). God commanded that no one take the life of another because life is good (Exod. 20:13). You can risk service to others when you trust, like Jesus, that you have come from God.

I became an adult in the self-esteem era, circa 1970 to 1980. The mantra was "I'm OK. You're OK." Clergy, counselors, and educators tried to get everyone to feel good about themselves. I, however, was never good at self-talk. Sessions in front of the mirror only reminded me of my shortcomings and flabby figure. During those days of intense effort to find ways to like ourselves—which I always thought was a little circuitous—I came to the conclusion that my worth did not stem from anything I could see in or say about myself. My confidence came from the truth that I was made by God, and the sacrifice of God's Son became the price tag on my life! Trusting that I had come from God and that God saw me as valuable enough to allow his only

Son to die for me gave me all the confidence I needed. You can have that same kind of confidence if you will quit looking in the mirror and start looking to God.

One way to know that you have come from God is to observe how God has molded you to be a unique servant leader. In the *Jesus on Leadership* workbook, we take two weeks to develop what I call your S.E.R.V.E. profile.[6] I gladly acknowledge Rick Warren's pioneering work in this area of helping people see how God has shaped them in order to find a place in ministry. I am indebted to him for the model of who we are in Christ Jesus. I consider these five aspects of your life the "raw materials" God uses to mold you into a unique servant leader. How Christ's teachings and examples play out in your life and calling comes from how God has uniquely made you. The scope of this work does not warrant a full discussion of each element, but I do want to address them briefly as they relate to our overall discussion of leadership.

1. Spiritual gifts are those gifts God gives through his holy spirit to empower you for service in the body of Christ.[7]

To receive God's grace for salvation is to receive God's gifts for service. Every member belongs in spiritually gifted ministry because every member is part of the living body of Christ. The image of the church as body changes how you do church. Stephen Covey declares that "the body is the best metaphor; it is the model organization."[8] (Once again, conventional wisdom declares the wisdom of God!) Bill Easum says that this picture of the church prevents any sense of control, the sacred cow of churches:

> Imagine a human body where all the parts must "get permission" before they can function. Or a healthy body

telling a kidney or heart to quit functioning on behalf
of the body. . . . These parts of the body function
automatically without any help from the brain. So it is
with most members and ministries in the Body of Christ.[9]

....

FILLING ORGANIZATIONAL CHARTS WITH
WARM BODIES WILL CERTAINLY KILL
A CHURCH. FREEING GOD'S PEOPLE TO
SERVE AS GOD HAS GIFTED THEM MAKES
A CHURCH GROW.

....

Filling organizational charts with warm bodies regardless
of heart attitude or spiritual giftedness will certainly kill a
church. Freeing God's people to serve as God has gifted them
to serve makes a church grow. Knowing how God has gifted
you for service in the body will give you the confidence to take
risks and pioneer new ministries.

We need to keep in mind an important distinction: Natural
giftedness for leadership is not the same as spiritual giftedness
for leadership. Natural giftedness is a mix of personality and
skill. Spiritual giftedness is God's empowerment, with a certain
expression of his Spirit, to lead within the body of Christ. Natural leadership gifts do not guarantee the spiritual gift of leadership. Remember that King Saul, Israel's first king, had all the
natural gifts of leadership, but he lacked a heart for the things
of God. This latter aspect of Saul's life caused God to withdraw
his blessing from the king.

Another thing to keep in mind: God extends his call to leadership beyond those people who have a gift of leadership.

I want to encourage you in the event that you find yourself
in a place of leadership but with a spiritual gift other than
leadership. God makes leaders of those he calls to carry out

his mission in the church. Look at Gideon, Esther, Peter, and Paul. The power of God, not the natural giftedness of the person, makes a spiritual leader. If you are a pastor and have the gift of teaching, for example, take Bill Hybels's advice. Bill, himself a gifted pastor and leader, advises pastors to surround themselves with "Spirit-enabled leaders who are elders, deacons, or in the other positions of influence in the church. These people should be freed up to exercise their leadership gift while the pastor concentrates on transformational preaching."[10]

....

IF GOD HAS CALLED YOU TO A DIVINE MISSION, GOD WILL PROVIDE THE LEADERSHIP RESOURCES TO COMPLETE THAT MISSION.

....

If God has called you to a divine mission, God will provide the leadership resources to complete that mission. Look at King David's team of "mighty men" (2 Sam. 23:8). All leaders, no matter their giftedness, must have teams of leaders around them, or they will lead alone. And that is death for a leader. I know this. One of my primary gifts is teaching!

The Bible mentions two leadership gifts in its representative lists of spiritual gifts. Those are the gifts of leadership (Rom. 12:8) and administration (1 Cor. 12:28). Leadership comes from the context of the Greek politic. It means to stand in front of the assembly. Members with this leadership gift serve the church as those who stand in front of the assembled church and call the people to a common vision and goal. The leadership gift empowers members to help others see which hill to take. If this gift were a body part, it would be an eye. This gift fits the model of the leader as pioneer.

The second leadership gift in the church is administration. This gift does not mean that the person is organized. The meaning of this gift comes from the context of shipping in the ancient world. This person was the "steersman or pilot" of a boat or ship.[11] He was the helmsman. The pilot guided the ship to the chosen coordinates. He was most valued in times of storm. This gift is separate from apostle, prophet, and teacher, which implies that administration is not a speaking gift but a gift that provides direction and guidance. This gift would be the second eye in the body made up of many parts. With two eyes of leadership, one to see which hill to take and the other to see the way up the hill, a church can move forward in a unified way. This gift would fit Peter Senge's model of "leader as designer."[12]

If there are two leadership gifts, is leadership in the church limited to the people with these two gifts? As I search the New Testament, I find examples of leaders with a variety of spiritual gifts. Actually, no New Testament character is described as having the gift of leadership. We can go to the pages of the Bible with our ideas of what a natural or spiritual leader looks like and find examples of those kinds of people. The Bible simply tells us stories of how God spiritually empowered a variety of naturally gifted people to achieve divine, uncommon goals.

For example, Paul and Barnabas are listed among the prophets and teachers in Antioch (Acts 13:1). While Paul exhibited natural leadership gifts, he claimed to be only a teacher and preacher of the Good News. His favorite designation of himself was apostle and servant. I believe his leadership style, which we observe in Scripture, came more from his natural relational style than his spiritual giftedness. I would argue that Barnabas's primary gift was exhortation or encouragement, although he was clearly a leader in the early church. On the inaugural missionary journey to the Gentiles, the people of Lystra gave Barnabas the title of Zeus and Paul the title of

Hermes, Zeus's messenger (Acts 14:12). My take on the biblical record is that God chose all kinds of people to lead in the church and gifted them in a variety of ways.

....

SERVANT LEADERSHIP AS MODELED AND
TAUGHT BY JESUS ALLOWS FOR ANY GIFT
TO BE USED IN A LEADERSHIP ROLE.

....

Servant leadership as modeled and taught by Jesus allows for any gift to be used in a leadership role. Just as any one of the four personality types can be the core of a person's leadership style, any of the gifts subjected to the mission of Jesus can be used to lead during a season of the church's life.

2. Experience is the second raw material God uses to mold you into a unique servant leader.

Have you ever wondered why God allows bad things to happen to good people? Me too. Often, deacons or caregivers in our church ask me for resources to help a person understand why God took a loved one away from them. The crux of the matter seems to be whether or not God is really in control; and, if he is, why did he let such a horrible thing happen? My faith stance, based on the biblical record, is that God either allows or ordains events in our lives.[13] This is a definition founded on faith—a faith that admits that we can't see everything from God's perspective and that God's ways are ultimately redemptive. This kind of faith allows us to see God at work even in the worst circumstances. God's Son did die on the cross. Faith also permits us to be thankful for the tough times. These "dark nights of the soul" can be times when we learn most about ourselves and God. Failures become avenues of success we never imagined when we trust God to work through every event to mold us.

Events are God's crucible to mold you into Christ's likeness. I believe servant leaders learn to lead through experiences God allows in their lives. Leadership cannot be taught; it must be learned. The best laboratory for leadership is life itself.

The leader can and must learn from experience. Warren Bennis writes that learning from experience means

❖ looking back at your childhood and adolescence and using what happened to you then to enable you to make things happen now so that you become the master of your own life rather than its servant.

❖ consciously seeking the kinds of experiences in the present that will improve and enlarge you.

❖ taking risks as a matter of course, with the knowledge that failure is as vital as it is inevitable.

❖ seeing the future—yours and the world's—as an opportunity to do all those things you have not done and those things that need to be done, rather than as a trial or a test.[14]

Experiences, for God's leader, can become "spiritual markers" for the presence of God in your life. Henry Blackaby says that a spiritual marker "identifies a time of transition, decision, or direction when I clearly know that God has guided me."[15] Every follower of Jesus has times when he knows God has broken into history to guide him to a place of service or new level of relationship with God. These experiences are how God teaches Christlike leadership. They are also how we learn the heart and purposes of God.

One of my favorite writers is Madeleine L'Engle. In her recent novel, *A Live Coal in the Sea,* the main character, Camilla, tries to explain to her granddaughter, Raffi, how she has coped with hurt in her relationships. As she rehearses the most difficult

part of her life, she quotes for her granddaughter a saying that
has become her perspective. This insight helped her survive
the deepest hurts. Camilla tells Raffi of an encounter with an
unlikely friend Edward, who helped her see how she could overcome a significant hurt in her marriage to Art.

> He [Edward] reached across his desk to me, and took my
> hands. He told me that people make mistakes, but are
> not bound by them. He told me that Art and I would love
> each other more, not less. I sat there and wept because I
> thought I had lost Art forever, that he might as well be
> dead. Young Edward handed me his handkerchief, a clean
> linen square, and quoted to me something written around
> fourteen hundred, by William Langland. . . . "But all the
> wickedness in the world which man may do or think is
> no more to the mercy of God than a live coal dropped in
> the sea."[16]

The mercy of God swallows the evil of man as though it were
a live coal in the sea. Faith allows the servant leader to trust that
God's mercy and purposes are greater than any hurt inflicted by
others. This conviction makes it possible for servant leaders to
learn from every experience in order to become the leaders God
wants them to become.

Tools like John Trent's *LifeMapping*[17] or an instrument for
writing your personal timeline can be used to discover how
God has guided your life to accomplish his purposes. When seen
through the eyes of faith, your life experiences cease to be your
story and become His-story.

3. Your relational style is another aspect of how God has molded you into a unique servant leader.[18]

God has wired you temperamentally as part of his plan for your life. This temperament is core to who you are and how you function. Knowing this aspect of yourself will help you develop and live out a personal leadership style.

My primary source for understanding behavioral theory is the guidance and teaching from my friend Ken Voges, who has written *Understanding How Others Misunderstand You*.[19] He also designed the "Relationship Survey" found in the *Jesus on Leadership* workbook.[20] Ken uses the letters *DISC* to represent the four primary relational styles. *D* stands for "dominance" style, *I* stands for the "influencing" style, *S* is the "steadiness" style, and *C* represents the "conscientious" style. This four-category model has been proven over time and has strong scientific support. This behavioral theory is used often by other Christian writers. Here's how the DISC model compares to others based on similar theories.

DISC	**Smalley/Trent**[21]	**LaHaye**[22]
Dominance	Lion	Choleric
Influencing	Otter	Sanguine
Steadiness	Golden Retriever	Phlegmatic
Conscientious	Beaver	Melancholic

These relational styles are ingrained in who we are. To understand these patterns of behavior is to understand our natural tendencies when relating to others.

No one temperament is superior for leadership among God's people. Once again, as we search the Scriptures we see that God chose people with all four primary styles. God chose Moses, who had a conscientious relational style with which he related the holiness and purposes of God in the details of the Law. God commissioned Abraham, who desired things to stay the same and who hated conflict, to leave his home on a journey without maps. God called Peter, who had a natural ability to influence others, to lead the church in Jerusalem. God redirected Paul's dominant, task-oriented style of relating to others to carry out the worldwide mission of taking the gospel to the ends of the earth.[23]

....

GOD DIDN'T GO LOOKING FOR LEADERS.
GOD LOOKED FOR OBEDIENT PEOPLE,
WHOM HE THEN FORMED INTO LEADERS.

....

Each of these relational styles became leadership styles when God called that person to lead. *God did not go looking for leaders. God looked for obedient people, whom he then formed into leaders*— though some went kicking and screaming (remember Gideon!).

Gary Smalley contends that personality types are a "key to lovability" in relationships.

> We're all a blend of four basic personality types, but most of us have one or two dominant styles. Our individual blends make us unique, like fingerprints. And one of the best ways to improve our relationships is to bring balance to any of our traits that we've neglectfully or subconsciously pushed to an extreme.[24]

I agree with Smalley that better understanding of motivations and actions that grow out of our basic personality can help us reach personal and marital satisfaction. Knowing your own personality type will help you know your natural tendencies in facing change and making day-to-day decisions.

After leading through change and being in the people business, I am convinced that the majority of conflicts—in the church, home, and marketplace—arise out of relational style differences. We simply see things differently because we are wired differently. As I have led our church, I have encountered conflict. Every leader does. Most of those conflicts were the result of personality differences, not theological ones. My personality style thrives on change. Other styles crave the status quo. Imagine the conflicts that arise over the issue of how decisions are made in an organization. Some people prefer quick decisions made within a flat organization. Others prefer well-thought-out decisions within a system of checks and balances. Resolution comes when we take time to listen and understand each other. Leadership happens when we move forward in the same direction and in a spirit of cooperation.

Effective leaders understand their own natural tendencies first and then take time to understand as best they can the relational strengths and weaknesses of those who follow them. An effective leader's greatest act of service to those who are on his team is to create an environment in which natural strengths can flourish and weaknesses can be compensated for.

4. God also uses your vocational skills as raw materials for servant leadership.[25]

I believe that whatever vocational skills you have learned can be invested in the mission of the church. Paul invested his ability to interpret Scripture and make tents in the mission to the ethnics. Lydia invested her business skills to support part of God's mission to reach people like herself (Acts 16:11-15). Aquila and Priscilla invested their tentmaking skills into Paul's mission in Corinth. After Paul had trained them, he left them in Ephesus to build up the church there (Acts 18). My vocational skills revolve around speaking, biblical studies, languages, and writing. Those make up my skill base to contribute to the mission of the church.

Billy Allen sells basketball shoes. He was an outstanding player at Southern Methodist University and played in the Continental Basketball Association for two years after college. Billy and his wife, Lisa, are also on mission with us at Legacy. Billy came to me after a message about investing vocational skills in the work of God. He said he conducted basketball clinics and wondered if that fit into the work of the church. I said, "You bet it does!" Four months later, we had our first Legacy Drive Baptist Church Skills and Drills Basketball Camp at the local YMCA. Three men and two women took off three days from work to coach fifty ten- to twelve-year-olds on the basics of basketball. We also took time each day to share our faith in Jesus. We reached families we would have not reached otherwise because Billy invested his talents in the work of God.

You have skills that you can put to use in reaching and ministering to people in the name of Christ. Make a list of skills you have learned either from formal training or while pursuing a hobby. Prayerfully look through that list, and imagine ways you can invest those skills into the work of meeting the needs of others. Whatever your list is—from computer programming to gardening—you can invest each skill into the work of God. We limit God when we do not invest all God has blessed us with.

5. Enthusiasm is the last raw material God uses to mold you into a unique servant leader.[26]

Enthusiasm is the passion God puts in your heart for his work. While this word is not in the original language of the New Testament, it represents the passion of God in a person's life. I am learning that this passion comes with a true calling; a person motivated by God's goals is always more enthusiastic than a person maintaining the status quo. The sense of mission becomes an all-consuming passion for the servant leader. Once we have humbled ourselves before God's call on our lives, that call, in turn, becomes the wellspring of passion that makes us true leaders.

Why was Jesus a passionate leader? He could do nothing but be the Suffering Servant Messiah, the mission given him by his Father in heaven. Why was the apostle Paul a passionate leader? He could do nothing but the mission to carry the Good News to ethnics around the world. How can you become a passionate servant leader? Accept without compromise the call of God on your life.

After we began the construction of our third building in nine years, I "checked out." God had done a marvelous work in the life of our church to call us to join him in the harvest. This building was the last of four goals we had set to participate in the harvest around us. Once we had begun to reach each of our goals and the building began at the end of August, I lost focus. My enthusiasm was gone.

One day in October of that same year, a friend and leader of our personnel team asked me to breakfast. At that meal, he asked me the most important leadership question I have ever been forced to answer: "What is your passion, Gene?" Tom did not allow me to tell what I wanted or what I desired my passion to be. Tom wanted to know what drove me and why I was doing what I was doing. During that hour and a half meeting, God rekindled my passion for his mission. Buildings and goals had gotten in the way of making disciples. My enthusiasm had drained because I had gotten off mission and had focused on short-term goals rather than eternal purposes. Since that breakfast, my enthusiasm for ministry and being the pastor of a mission outpost has returned. Why? Because I realized again that it was the mission that made me get up in the morning and sleep well at night. (It also gave me focus for writing this book. This is what I am learning while on mission.)

....

MY ENTHUSIASM HAD DRAINED BECAUSE
I HAD GOTTEN OFF MISSION AND HAD
FOCUSED ON SHORT-TERM GOALS RATHER
THAN ON ETERNAL PURPOSES.

....

Here are the questions of enthusiasm: "What makes your heart beat fast?" and, "If you could do one thing for God, what would it be?" The answer to those questions will tell you the source of your enthusiasm for ministry.

YOU ARE RETURNING TO GOD

The final reality that will give us confidence to risk being servants is that we, like Jesus, are returning to God. Jesus' confession on the cross, "Father, into your hands I commit my spirit" (Luke 23:46), demonstrates that he trusted he was returning to his Father in heaven. Jesus came to teach us that we are all returning to God. His death and resurrection are the assurance that when we return to God we will receive God's mercy rather than God's wrath. His Holy Spirit is the earnest money that guarantees we will receive our inheritance (Eph. 1:13-14).

Trusting that you are returning to God gives you an eternal perspective. This perspective gives you a genuine sense of humor. You can smile throughout life because you know the punch line! If you trust only in things perishable, you cannot risk those things because they are all you have. I like the T-shirt slogan "Those who die with the most toys . . . still die." The sad truth of this is that if returning to your Creator is not your life goal, then all you have to live for is accumulation of stuff. Your hope is only in things that you cannot take with you.

Trusting that God controls your eternity gives you the confidence to risk everything earthly to achieve anything eternal. The hope of a servant leader who follows Jesus is in an eternal relationship with the God who created you and sent his Son to die for you.

We live in a world that places value on things according to their price tags. Diamonds are more valuable than silver because you pay more for them. Pick almost any category of life, and price equals value. Christians should never value things the way the world does. Followers of Jesus should have an eternal perspective; our confidence that we are returning to our Creator—who laid down his life for us so we can spend eternity with him—is our most valuable commodity.

My youngest daughter loves dolls . . . and friends and dogs and gerbils and finches. One day I mishandled one of her dolls. She barked out, "Don't treat my doll that way. It cost!" I apologized. Dads aren't so sensitive to the ways of doll care. I then challenged her reasoning. I told her I would prefer to handle her doll differently because she thought it was a special doll rather than because of its price tag. We agreed that what things cost seem to tell how valuable they are. I asked her which was more valuable to her: her two finches that cost $12.95 each or the doll. She confessed that the finches meant more. She then allowed me to teach her a phrase we repeated together: "Price alone does not determine value."

Christians can have a proper perspective about things and position on earth because they know their true value comes from belonging to God. The trust that you will return to God will give you the peace you need to face the trials of leadership and life.

How do you risk your place at the head table to serve others? Let's summarize.

1. You trust that in your relationship with Christ you have all power to carry out God's call on your life.

2. You trust that you have come from God. God is the source of life for you. Among other things God has gifted you for service among his people and allowed experiences to mold you. He is using your vocational skills and motivating you through natural enthusiasm for God's purposes and plans.

3. You trust that at the end of this life you will return to the God who created you and that you will receive the

inheritance of eternal life he has promised you. This trust allows you to risk anything earthly for everything eternal.

You can risk the kind of leadership that humbly serves others if you trust God to be in control of your life. You believe that all you have is a gift and that God is the giver. You push away from the head table because you know that if God wants you there, God will make sure you get back there in his timing.

FOR STUDY AND REFLECTION

- Do you consider yourself a risk taker? If so, give some examples. If not, list some reasons.

- Jesus could risk service to others because he trusted that "all authority in heaven and on earth" had been given to him. How confident are you of that truth in your life? If it were true, how would it make you more confident to serve others?

- Jesus also trusted that he had come from God, the Father. Do you believe this for your life? If so, explain how that gives you confidence to serve others.

- We talked about developing your S.E.R.V.E. profile. Make a list of those parts of the profile you already know: spiritual gifts, experiences, relational style, vocational skills, enthusiasm. Seek to understand the others as God leads you.

- Jesus also trusted that he was returning to God. Do you trust that this is true for you? How can this give you confidence to risk serving others as Jesus did?

- Summarize the fourth principle of servant leadership. List three ways you can implement this principle in your life this week.

Endnotes on Principle #4

1. James M. Kouzes and Barry Z. Posner, *The Leadership Challenge* (New York: Warner Books, 1994), 8.

2. Joel Arthur Barker, *Future Edge* (New York: William Morrow, 1992), 71.

3. Steven F. Hayward, *Churchill on Leadership* (Rocklin, Calif.: Prima, 1997), 28–9.

4. Max DePree, *Leading without Power* (San Francisco: Jossey-Bass, 1997), 138.

5. Doug Murren, *Leadershift* (Ventura, Calif.: Regal, 1994), 128. Italics mine.

6. C. Gene Wilkes, *Jesus on Leadership* (Nashville: LifeWay Press, 1996), 31–84. S.E.R.V.E. is an acrostic for Spiritual Gifts, Experiences, Relational Style, Vocational Skills, and Enthusiasm. Rick Warren's acrostic S.H.A.P.E., which predates mine, stands for Spiritual Gifts, Heart Motivations, Abilities, Personality, Experiences.

7. Ibid., 35–48. A spiritual-gift inventory is included in the workbook.

8. Stephen Covey, *Principle-Centered Leadership* (New York: Simon and Schuster, 1992), 185.

9. William M. Easum, *Sacred Cows Make Gourmet Burgers* (Nashville: Abingdon, 1995), 45.

10. Lynn and Bill Hybels, *Rediscovering the Church* (Grand Rapids: Zondervan, 1995), 193.

11. Arndt and Gingrich, 457. See also Kubernsi (*Theological Dictionary of the New Testament,* vol. 3, 1035).

12. Peter Senge, *The Fifth Discipline* (New York: Doubleday, 1990), 341–5.

13. Wilkes, *Jesus on Leadership,* 49–56.

14. Warren Bennis, *On Becoming a Leader* (Reading, Mass.: Addison-Wesley, 1994), 99–100.

15. Henry Blackaby and Claude King, *Experiencing God* (Nashville: LifeWay Press, 1990), 101.

16. Madeleine L'Engle, *A Live Coal in the Sea* (New York: HarperCollins, 1997), 167.

17. John Trent, *LifeMapping* (Colorado Springs: Focus on the Family, 1994).

18. Wilkes, *Jesus on Leadership,* 57–72. A "Relational Style Survey" is included as part of the workbook. I am indebted to my friend Ken Voges for my understanding of the four personality types and the biblical characters that represent them.

19. Ken Voges and Ron Braund, *Understanding How Others Misunderstand You* (Chicago: Moody Press, 1990).

20. Wilkes, *Jesus on Leadership,* 60–1.

21. Gary Smalley and John Trent, *The Two Sides of Love* (Colorado Springs: Focus on the Family, 1990), 34–6.

22. Tim LaHaye, *Spirit-Controlled Temperament* (Wheaton, Ill.: Tyndale House, 1966).

23. The female counterparts are Esther, Hannah, Abigail, and Lydia respectively.

24. Gary Smalley, *Making Love Last Forever* (Waco, Tex.: Word, 1996), 159.

25. Wilkes, *Jesus on Leadership,* 73–9.

26. Ibid., 80–3.

TAKE UP THE TOWEL

LEADERS live the vision by making all their actions and behaviors consistent with it and by creating a sense of urgency and passion for its attainment.
BURT NANUS *Visionary Leadership*

IN WASHING the feet of the disciples, Christ gave an example of love, for this is the nature of love—to serve and to be subject to one another.
MARTIN LUTHER *Book of Jesus*

WHEN Jesus tied a towel around his waist, poured water into a copper basin, and washed the feet of the apostles, the Maundy Thursday revolution began, and a new idea of greatness in the Kingdom of God emerged.
BRENNAN MANNING *Signature of Jesus*

AS THE cross is the sign of submission, so the towel is the sign of service.
RICHARD J. FOSTER *Celebration of Discipline*

JESUS performed two symbolic acts for his followers on the night he was betrayed. This was his last opportunity to make sure his leadership team understood his mission. It was his last chance to see if they could complete the mission after he left. On the night of his betrayal, Jesus took bread and wine from the Passover meal and showed himself to be the final sacrifice to take away the sins of the world. He also took up a servant's towel and washbasin and washed his disciples' feet. Most Christians are familiar with the power and meaning of the first act, but what was his message in the second?

Luke tells us that after the Passover meal Jesus' followers began to discuss who was the greatest in the group (Luke 22:24). This was a common topic with his followers. But I think we ought to cut them some slack. They were, after all, guys! Guys always seem to get into discussions about who caught the biggest fish or closed the largest deal. Pastor guys are notorious for telling their fellow ministers they had at least 10 percent more people at an event than were really there. We reward this behavior when we give the biggest jobs to the guys with the biggest stories.

I think the disciples were simply sharing stories about how God had worked through them. They had forgotten, however, that it was God and not them who did the work! The last week in Jerusalem had been tough, but they had seen Jesus attack the religious leaders. Jesus had also made great strides in winning over the people. These kingdom seekers thought the signs for victory were good. So they began to discuss who would sit at Jesus' side when he came into his kingdom again. Jesus surprised his followers when he left the head table (while they argued about who would sit where) and moved to where servants worked. He wrapped a towel around his waist, filled a basin with water, and began to wash the dusty feet of his friends.

Our fifth principle of servant leadership is based upon Jesus' washing of his disciples feet:

Servant leaders take up Jesus' towel of servanthood to meet the needs of others.

From this event we understand that Jesus' towel of servanthood is the physical symbol of servant leadership. His act to meet the physical and spiritual needs of his followers shows us what servant leaders do.

Washing feet was not Jesus' job. He was teacher and master. No one would criticize a leader who delegated such a menial task to another member of the group. We think, *Leaders deal with the big issues. You hire others to do the lowly tasks.* Once again we face a paradox of servant leadership. If you are given the task of stewarding the vision and mission of the group and you are responsible for completing the mission, why would you "get off task" to do something so small as washing feet? Jesus the leader confused our thinking when he became Jesus the servant. Why would the King of kings wear a towel to wash others' feet?

Yet when we watch Jesus take up the towel of servanthood, we notice two things. First, he demonstrated that servant leaders meet the needs of the group in order to carry out the mission. Jesus' followers had dirty feet, and no one was willing to wash them. The group had a need, but no one would leave his place to meet it. They were too busy comparing themselves to one another.

This mentality affects how families and organizations function. "It's not my job" is an attitude that prevents cooperation and teamwork. In a family, this attitude usually enslaves one member of the family to washing clothes and cleaning the house or tending to all the child care. In a business, the same attitude will kill any sense of teamwork. Have you ever had a staff member who made it very clear what was and was not her job? Did this person refuse to do anything other than what was in her job description? When "it's not my job" thinking enters a staff, teamwork is impaired. Territories are marked out and defended. Battles are fought over who does what and who does more than the others. But Jesus showed us that leaders with towels are willing to meet whatever need exists—regardless of whose job it is.

The second lesson Jesus provided when he washed feet was that dirty feet were not the real need. The disciples' discussion about greatness revealed their real need—to know who Jesus was and why he had come. Their continued display of head-table mentality revealed that they still did not fully understand why Jesus had come. He had come to *serve*. Any followers of his would be *servants*. On his last night with the disciples, Jesus had to emphasize once again what kind of kingdom they were part of—and what it would take for them to follow in his footsteps.

JESUS' POWER—
THROUGH SERVICE

"WHERE's the leadership in servant leadership?" is a question often asked when I speak about servant leadership. When I was finishing my work on the *Jesus on Leadership* workbook, the publishers asked several people to read its contents and make comments. One reader sent back the manuscript and asked, "Where is the leadership part? All I see is how Jesus served others. Point out how serving is part of leading." I was pleased that the reader had discovered this. The workbook (and this book) was supposed to describe the leadership style of Jesus. As I walked through all I had learned from observing Jesus, my thoughts returned again to the night Jesus washed the feet of his disciples. There Jesus modeled how leaders can be servants and still lead. When we look at the events of that night, we can usually see only a lot of service and no leading. We ask, "If you're serving all the time, where's the power?" Service and leadership seem to be opposing concepts. We think you cannot be one and do the other. We find the answers to this question as we watch Jesus' actions on the night he was betrayed.

He modeled the mission.

When Jesus left the table to take the form of a servant and do the work of a slave, he was providing a real-life picture of his mission. He had already taught that his mission was "not to be served, but to serve, and to give his life as a ransom for many" (Mark 10:45). His descent from his position of final Passover lamb to lowly servant paralleled his descent from heaven to the cross. Remember what he taught about humility? "He who humbles himself will be exalted" (Luke 14:11). Remember the hymn of humiliation and Jesus' exaltation by his Father? He "made himself nothing, taking the very nature of a servant" (Phil. 2:7). By moving from head table to lowest place in the group, Jesus offered a visual illustration of his life's mission.

Jesus' mission was to be the Suffering Servant of God. The Gospels tell how time and again Jesus had to correct his followers' perception of who he was as the Messiah. The five thousand people he fed wanted him to be a popular Messiah who would meet all their physical desires. Others, like James and John, wanted him to be a political Messiah who would set up an earthly kingdom. Simon, the Zealot, and his friends wanted Jesus to be a military Messiah who would throw off the yoke of Roman oppression. People still have these kinds of wishes and expectations attached to their faith in Jesus.

....

WE STILL WANT JESUS TO BE WHAT WE WANT HIM TO BE. BUT THOSE WHO FOLLOW A POPULAR MESSIAH ARE SOON DISAPPOINTED WHEN HE ASKS FOR SOMETHING IN RETURN.

....

We still want Jesus to be what we want him to be. When we take a stand for Jesus, we want him to be popular with those who know and accept us. We want Jesus to feed our hungers and fulfill our wishes. We want him to heal our diseases and fix our marriages. We join the five thousand who wanted to make him king because he gave them lunch. Those who follow a popular Messiah are soon disappointed when he asks something in return for their allegiance.

Others still want Jesus to be a political Messiah. You don't have to look far to find Christians who want to set up the kingdom of God by electing Christians to political office. While Jesus taught us to be salt and light, he personally rejected any ideas of making himself a political leader. Jesus never ran for public office. His was a spiritual kingdom. Those whom God calls to public service must continually check their view of government against that of the One who called them. The problem with wanting Jesus to be a political messiah is that your faith is shattered when God allows anyone other than those you put on the ticket to be elected.

Finally, some still want Jesus to be a military Messiah. While this temptation is not as prevalent in the United States, we know many Christians who hold to a liberation theology that allows Jesus to carry a machine gun and overthrow governments with revolutionary forces. I think it is significant that Jesus chose Simon the Zealot to be one of the Twelve. Simon was part of the revolutionary Jewish movement sworn to remove Rome from their soil. I believe Jesus called Simon in order to challenge his faith in military action to accomplish the will of God. The disciple surely struggled with the Sermon on the Mount. When you hope for war, loving your enemies and turning the other cheek are "childspeak." Simon must not have slept well the night of his Savior's death. If he had hoped a cavalry of angels (or men) would have come and rescued Jesus from the Roman war machine, he must have truly been disappointed. I wish I could have been there when the resurrected Lord explained the true power of his kingdom to Simon before he ascended into heaven.

....

TOO MANY LEADERS FAIL WHEN THEY LEAVE THE MISSION TO PLEASE THEIR FOLLOWERS.

....

Jesus, however, was the Suffering Servant Messiah. His mission was to be the fulfillment of Isaiah's prophecy about the kind of Messiah God would send to free his people. The prophet said, "After the suffering of his soul, he will see the light of life and be satisfied; by his knowledge my righteous servant will justify many, and he will bear their iniquities" (Isa. 53:11). Jesus' mission was not to fulfill the wishes of those who followed him. His mission was to carry out the will of the Father. *Too many leaders fail when they leave the mission to please their followers.* This is why Jesus continually corrected his disciples when they (Peter, in particular) tried to keep him from suffering and dying to bring salvation to his people. His mission was to lay down his life as a sacrifice to bring a right relationship between God and all creation. His followers had to understand his mission before they could understand their own.

As Jesus knelt before his disciples and washed their feet, he gave them a picture of his mission. He came to serve. He came to suffer.

He modeled his teachings.

Jesus had already taught the principles of servant leadership to his followers. Now he modeled those principles. He taught his followers to take the lowest place when invited to a banquet (Luke 14:10). He now modeled humility by taking up the towel of a servant. He had been teaching that greatness among God's people came through becoming a servant (Mark 10:43-44). He now modeled that kind of greatness by dressing like a servant. Jesus had taught that being first in line meant becoming a slave to others. He now modeled being first by doing the work of a slave. Our teachings take on incredible power when we back them up by our actions.

Many parents fail their children by teaching them one thing and modeling something else. We teach our children to be honest— no matter what. One day a woman called and asked if one of my daughters would sit with her children on a Monday night. I did not know the woman, and school nights are not the best times for students to be out late. My daughter, with her hand over the mouthpiece, asked me what she should say. I said, "Tell her you have gym that night." (She goes to gym two nights a week.) My daughter hesitated but told the mother her excuse and hung up. The next day I was driving in the car with my daughter. I remembered the "white lie" I had told her to tell. I told her I had wronged her because I had asked her to lie. I also asked her to forgive me and said that she was not to let me do it the next time I tried that again! She smiled and forgave me. Leaders in any position lose credibility when their actions do not square with their teaching.

Jesus led by modeling his mission and his teachings for those who argued about who was greatest in the group. His teachings and his actions were in sync. Those who follow him can always know that what he said and how he acted match.

Dressed like a servant, acting like a slave—Jesus still led.

When Jesus came to Peter's dirty feet, his close friend refused his service. Peter said, "You shall never wash my feet" (John 13:8). This was a noble response from a leader in the group, but why did he say what he did?

First of all, I think Peter may have been embarrassed that he had not thought to do the job his leader was now doing. Peter was sensitive that way—always the first to please his leader. He was the first to step from the boat onto the rocky waves. He was the first to declare Jesus to be the Christ. Peter wanted to please

Jesus that night as Jesus knelt before him. He was embarrassed to let his leader down. He was probably reprimanding himself for not noticing the need and doing something about it.

I also believe Peter's reaction was consistent with his refusal to allow his Messiah to suffer. Peter's Messiah would not do the work of a slave! The lead disciple refused to accept anything that was less than his personal perception of the mission. His leader would never wash his feet because that was below the leader's dignity and position. Peter held to the misconception that leaders never do small things.

Kneeling before Peter's smelly feet and wearing the towel of service, Jesus revealed his disciple's lack of understanding for the mission. Peter still did not understand Jesus' mission on earth. His refusal revealed his confusion. Sometimes a leader must reveal a need before he can meet that need.

Peter's refusal of Jesus' offering was an obstacle to the Savior's path to the cross. Peter offered a "shortcut to the kingdom," which Jesus refused. This was not the first time Peter had revealed his own perception of what the kingdom should be. At Cesarea Philippi, Jesus called Peter "Satan" because the disciple offered Jesus the kingdom without suffering (Mark 8:29-33). Jesus had to lead in the face of opposition. "Leaders learn by leading, and they learn best by leading in the face of obstacles,"[1] advises Warren Bennis. Leaders also lead in the face of criticism. Jesus continued to lead, kneeling at Peter's feet, although he faced opposition from one of his closest followers.

. . . .

JESUS LED WITHOUT GIVING IN
TO THE PERSONAL PREFERENCES OF
HIS FOLLOWERS. SOMETIMES A LEADER
MUST REVEAL A NEED BEFORE HE
CAN MEET THAT NEED.

. . . .

This encounter between Jesus and Peter at the Passover meal also teaches us that *Jesus led without giving in to the personal preferences of his followers.* Meeting others' needs does not mean giving in to people's wishes. Jesus knelt as a servant at Peter's feet, but he did not allow Peter's personal preferences about who he was as Messiah to keep him from his appointed mission. Peter did not get his way. Jesus said, "Unless I wash you, you have no part with me" (John 13:8). He meant that either Peter accepted Jesus' mission of Messiah as Jesus defined it or Peter was no longer part of the movement. Servant leadership does not lack resolve. Servant leaders do not waver from their appointed mission just because one of their followers has another idea of how things should be.

When one becomes servant to the mission, that mission becomes the resolve that is the basis of strong leadership during critical times. Unwavering resolve in the face of challenge does not come from personality alone. One's resolve to lead is directly proportional to one's service to the mission. Leaders falter in the face of challenge when they do not have or fully understand the mission.

I have told you how God's call to mission in my life and our church has become central to my motivation to lead. I did not lead well before I realized that call on my life. When I was in college, I belonged to a service organization. At the end of my junior year, I thought I would run for president of the club. I remember two influential seniors telling me they would support a friend of mine because I was not a leader. That, as you can imagine, was a blow to my ego. Their influence prevailed because I was elected sergeant at arms! I accepted their assessment and waited for a time to prove my leadership. When I look back on those days, I have to agree with my friends. I was not a leader. I would falter in the face of challenge and wait to see what the group wanted to do before I would step up to lead.

Without mission, there was no resolve to lead. With God's call on my life—and responsibility for the people I am entrusted with—I am learning to lead.

Jesus was a resolute servant leader because he had become an absolute servant to God's call on his life. Popular opinion and personal preference did not cause him to falter from his calling. *This is why, on that night, the banner of the kingdom was a towel stained with dirt.*

....

ON THAT NIGHT, THE BANNER OF THE KINGDOM WAS A TOWEL STAINED WITH DIRT.

....

He passed the ultimate test of servanthood.

I have read the story of Jesus' washing his disciples' feet many times. A couple of years ago, I read beyond the event and teachings of Jesus on that night. It struck me as it never had before that Jesus washed Judas's feet, too.[2] Jesus washed the feet of the disciple who would betray him with a kiss later that night. Knowing that Judas would turn him over to the religious leaders—an act that would result in Jesus' death—the Lord still washed Judas's feet. By doing so, Jesus passed what I believe to be the greatest test of a servant leader.

Jesus' washing Judas's feet still baffles me. My natural tendencies would say, "If you knew the guy was a traitor, why didn't you get rid of him?" Others would judge, "If you were a good leader, Jesus, you would have known what was going on and stopped it from happening." Those, however, are statements of people who are protecting a head-table position. *Servants who live out the will of their Father in heaven do not fear human schemes.* Their confidence is in the purposes of God, not their efforts to control circumstances.

The picture is amazing. Here was the King of kings kneeling before the one who had already sold him to the enemy for thirty pieces of silver. They both knew the deal was done. Both knew the end result. Still Jesus did not skip Judas when it came his turn to be washed. Judas had a need—as all the others did. He, too, must see his Savior kneeling at his feet before he saw him hanging on a cross. Only love beyond human capacity can motivate a leader to humble himself before a person who may be turning him over to his enemies.

....

SERVANTS WHO LIVE OUT THE WILL OF THEIR FATHER IN HEAVEN DO NOT FEAR HUMAN SCHEMES.

....

As with Peter, Jesus did not let Judas go without addressing his need. Jesus did not let his mission cave in to the opposition's schemes to destroy him. When Peter accepted Jesus' gift of service, Jesus said, "A person who has had a bath needs only to wash his feet; his whole body is clean. And you are clean, though not every one of you" (John 13:10). Jesus was referring to Judas when he said "not every one of you." With that comment, we see Jesus expose the sin of betrayal while still serving the sinner. Jesus kept Judas accountable for his misdeed, but he still washed his feet. Amazing grace.

I believe your greatest test as a servant leader may be to wash the feet of those who may soon betray you. Leaders will always be tested by those who seek their position or want to push their own agenda. Leaders must continually address those who try to refocus the group's attention. Every group can have a Judas who will force the leader's hand to act according to the traitor's wishes. The resolve of a servant leader will be activated at the point of this challenge.

But the greatest test of your leading with the heart of Jesus is not whether or not you overcome the challenges of others. It is whether or not you serve those who have the power to take you out. We honor Jesus because he washed his betrayer's feet. That was nothing. Honor goes to Jesus because the next day he died in the place of his betrayer. If you are willing to climb on a cross for someone because you love him, washing his dirty feet is a walk in the park.

I learned this lesson when God drove me to my knees to wash the feet of my chairman of deacons (in the story I told at the beginning of this book). I am no hero for washing Ted's feet. If, months before, I had been a servant leader like Jesus, foot washing in those circumstances would not have been necessary. As it turned out, that was a moment of grace orchestrated by God. That act, and more so Ted's reciprocal act of washing my feet, revealed the heart of Jesus to me.

Jesus did not come to gain a place of power.

He did not come to defeat his human enemies.

He did not come to overthrow an unjust government.

Jesus came to show us the heart of God. His entire message and ministry on earth was to show selfish, power-hungry people like you and me what love looks like. As he knelt before Judas, Jesus showed us a love that no human can conceive on his own: a love that is brutally honest about what is going on but still kneels before us to lay down his life so we can be free from the sin that infects us. Jesus loves you as he loved Judas. If you miss that, you have missed eternal life.

HOW DO WE LEAD AS SERVANTS?

HOW do we take the example of Jesus into our lives? Let me try some answers. The servant leader will model his mission, model what he teaches, lead while dressed like a servant and acting like a slave, and be able to pass the greatest test of servant leadership.

Provide a picture of your mission.
Your actions will be your most valuable tool in casting a vision and staying the course. Kouzes and Posner, authors of *The Leadership Challenge*, write:

> Modeling the way is how leaders make their visions tangible. It is the brick and mortar, nails and lumber, carpeting and furniture, electrical outlets and placement of windows, and all of the hundreds of other details that go into realizing the architect's model of a new home.[3]

To model the mission is to act out what you are calling your followers to do. This is why I wash deacons' feet and give towels to those we ordain. Of course, those would be empty symbols if I were not willing to carry out the trash or help move furniture.

I have a towel in my office with shoe polish on it. I normally use it when we set apart members of our church as deacons. Each time we set someone aside for ministry, I get on my knees and wipe the dust from the servants' shoes in front of the gathered church. I do this for two reasons: (1) I do this to remind myself of my role as the church's servant leader. Jesus washed feet and commanded me to do the same. (2) I want each of those whom we are setting apart to remember Jesus' example of servant leadership when he washed his disciples' feet.

Live out what you teach.

Joseph Stowell, the president of Moody Bible Institute, reminds church leaders to use their visibility as a leader to their advantage. In his book *Shepherding the Church into the Twenty-First Century,* I like his chapter title: "A Career in Modeling: Turning the Fishbowl to Christ's Advantage."[4] He reminds leaders that it is "our visibility that gives us viability in the work. . . . When our visibility casts positive and compelling images, it is to our advantage since it platforms our capacity for effectiveness."[5] Modeling what you teach adds weight to your lessons.

Nan is the leader of our missions team. Her team is responsible for leading our church in missions locally and around the world. Nan came to me one day and said she no longer wanted to be on the team. She was tired of meeting and making decisions. She wanted to *do* missions, not decide *about* missions. She was tired of just teaching about missions; she wanted to learn about missions. We talked long about her concerns and agreed that if she and the team actually did missions, others would want to be part of living out Christ's great commission to make disciples of all ethnic groups.

The next summer Nan, another member, and a family from our church invested their time over the Fourth of July weekend to go to the Rio Grande region of Texas. They took a trailer full of items the church had collected during Vacation Bible School that summer. They held their own VBS in a small border town. Nan remained the leader of the missions team that year. She began to model what she had taught about missions. When others saw her example, they began to desire to be part of a team that sent people around the world to meet the needs of others.

You will lead others as you model what you teach. If all you have to offer are words, few people will follow you. Your example will give them a picture of what you are talking about.

....

IF ALL YOU HAVE TO OFFER ARE WORDS,
FEW PEOPLE WILL FOLLOW YOU. YOUR
EXAMPLE WILL GIVE THEM A PICTURE OF
WHAT YOU ARE TALKING ABOUT.

....

Recognize the need—and take up the towel.

Servant leaders willingly leave their place at the head table to meet the needs of others. We don't see much of this these days. We tend to assign perks rather than lowly tasks to those at the head tables of our culture. But true servant leaders lead with stained towels and on dirty knees.

President Jimmy Carter is one of my heroes. He's a hero because he is a man of character who did not let the modern office of president of the United States of America distract him from his commitment to follow Jesus. I don't understand politics, foreign policy, or economics enough to evaluate Mr. Carter on those grounds. I guess if President Clinton can take credit for the booming economy while he is president, President Carter must take it on the chin for 22 percent interest rates during his administration. If President Bush can be honored by his leadership during the Gulf War, President Carter must take the blame for the botched effort to free the hostages in Iran. Sometimes leaders get credit and blame for things outside their control.

While I am not an astute student of politics, I do understand the power of taking up the towel of service. After his defeat by Ronald Reagan in 1980, I watched as President and Mrs. Carter began work with Habitat for Humanity. I was amazed that a man of such high office would seemingly lower himself to be part of building homes for those who could not afford them. I knew such behavior was part of his Christian character that motivated him to teach a Sunday school class even while he was president.

In his book *Living Faith,* President Carter tells how Jesus' example leads us to live a life of service toward others. Reflecting on Jesus' washing his disciples' feet, he wrote:

> This kind of image [Jesus' washing the disciples' feet] is profoundly important to me as I try, in my own way, to follow Jesus' example: for instance, when I go with a Habitat team to build a house in Los Angeles or Chicago, inhabited by the poorest Americans, surrounded by drug addicts and criminals, sometimes with gunfire resounding on nearby streets . . . the awareness that my God walked this way before me makes it possible to sustain such an effort.[6]

President Carter confessed that his motivation and model for joining the work of Habitat was the example of Jesus washing his disciples' feet. President and Mrs. Carter's work to build houses for the poor tells me they are servant leaders after the teaching and example of the one they call Lord. They willingly take up the towel to meet the needs of others.

Lead without giving in to the personal preferences of others.

Servant leadership means being servant to the mission and avoiding the temptation to please others. My natural personality wants others to like me. That motivates me to be kind and congenial. That same tendency also causes me to make decisions based on what people think of me. It was not until God got a hold on my heart with a vision for his church that I was able to lead beyond the personal preferences of others.

In 1992 we added a third service on Sunday morning. This service was a contemporary expression of what we believed. We offered the service out of a conviction that we needed to provide a worship experience for those who were not comfortable in a traditional church setting. We based our decision on our mission to make disciples, which meant beginning with lost people rather than with Christians. We made many changes in the appearance, style, and content of our worship services. Some people accepted these changes openly. Others were not one bit pleased. I learned that people often equate the style of worship with the orthodoxy of its content. Mission is set aside in favor of the familiar.

As I led through those days of transition, I faced opposition and criticism from those who preferred to worship a certain way. I also received many thanks from those who returned to church and those who longed for life in a worship experience. As I would sit with those who preferred the status quo, I felt that, because of the mission, I could not give in to others' preferences. Our mission was to reach those who did not understand our traditional ways of doing church. Changing the style of worship meant making a place for those we were trying to reach. Staying the course meant patiently telling members of our vision to become "a visible community of Christlike relationships, building a spiritual legacy of encouragement and hope" for those in our part of the world. Serving them while modeling the mission of our church allowed them to see our goal.

My personal journey has taught me that leadership means staying true to the mission, not necessarily to the wishes of the people—even the majority of the people. I now live by this axiom: "You cannot lead by consensus, but you must have consensus to lead." Consensus is a by-product, not a method, of good leadership. A 51 percent vote does not determine the will of God. A servant leader, however, gains the support of that 51 percent in order to complete the mission entrusted to the entire group. Personal preferences are secondary to divine purposes.

Be prepared to wash the feet of those who may soon betray you.

Servant leadership is the willingness to serve even those who have the ability to take you out. Jesus washed Judas's feet, too. The deacons of my church had the power to oust me. God used that experience to direct my heart toward service, rather than power, as my leadership style. My encounter with my deacon officers was a very hard time in my life. Given a choice, I would never have chosen to walk that road. God, however, used it to show me the depth of his love and how far he would stoop to serve the needs of sinful people—people who desired to make God into their own image.

....

YOUR GREATEST TEST AS A SERVANT
LEADER MAY BE TO WASH THE FEET OF
THOSE WHO MAY SOON BETRAY YOU.

....

If time allows, I tell every group I speak to the story of how God humbled me. I have talked to pastors and staff members who have told me sad stories of how churches have treated them. I do not know that washing the feet of those who are trying to take you out will end the way it did for me. But I do know that if you and I are going to lead like Jesus, we must be willing to risk whatever the consequences to model servant leadership. We can't forget that Jesus washed Judas's feet and was still betrayed by Judas and died on the cross. You don't wash feet to get your way. You wash feet because your Leader told you to wash feet.

LEAD FROM A KNEELING POSITION

Jesus said, "I have set you an example that you should do as I have done for you" (John 13:15). Those who lead in the kingdom of God must check where they sit and what they wear. If you are not kneeling at the feet of others, wearing a servant's towel, you are in the wrong place.

This example of Jesus does not fit the cultural picture of leadership. Jesus, however, did not come to show us a better way to do things. He came to show us how to live as kingdom people. Brennan Manning has captured the power of Jesus' example:

> What a shocking reversal of our culture's priorities and values! To prefer to be the servant rather than the lord of the household, to merrily taunt the gods of power, prestige, honor and recognition, to refuse to take oneself seriously, to live without gloom by a lackey's agenda; these are the attitudes and actions that bear the stamp of authentic discipleship. In effect, Jesus said: Blessed are you if you love to be unknown and regarded as nothing. All things being equal, to prefer contempt to honor, to prefer ridicule to praise, to prefer humiliation to glory— those are formulas of greatness in the new Israel of God.[7]

Those who lead in God's kingdom lead from a kneeling position, dressed like a servant. Before Jesus led the group to the garden for prayer that night, he promised that if they would do what he commanded them to do, they would be blessed (John 13:17).

Blessed be those who take up the towel in the name of Jesus.

FOR STUDY AND REFLECTION

- You and I are like Peter: we want to please Jesus, but we have our own perceptions of what he should be for us. After reading this chapter, what are some of your personal desires of Jesus? How does Jesus dressed like a servant and acting like a slave challenge your picture of Jesus?

- What are you doing to model your group's mission before the members of the team? Does what you do support what you say?

- List three things you can do this week to reinforce something you have taught your group.

- Make a list of personal preferences of those who follow you. Do some want you to be more popular? more powerful? How can you show them the true nature of God's mission for your life while continuing to serve?

- Who is the Judas on your team? What can you do to serve him or her in order to model the love of Jesus?

Endnotes for Principle #5

1. Warren Bennis, *On Becoming a Leader* (Reading, Mass.: Addison-Wesley, 1994), 146.

2. The order of events in the upper room is a topic of discussion in a different arena. Suffice it to say that John leaves the possibility of Judas's presence at the table open when he quotes Jesus: "though not every one of you" (John 13:10).

3. James M. Kouzes and Barry Z. Posner, *The Leadership Challenge* (San Francisco: Jossey-Bass, 1987), 190.

4. Joseph M. Stowell, *Shepherding the Church into the Twenty-First Century* (Colorado Springs: Victor, 1994), 102.

5. Ibid., 103.

6. Jimmy Carter, *Living Faith* (New York: Times Books, 1996), 233.

7. Brennan Manning, *The Signature of Jesus,* rev. ed. (Sisters, Oreg.: Multnomah, 1996), 100–1.

SHARE RESPONSIBILITY AND AUTHORITY

ONE sentence sums up the focus of Jesus' time
on earth: "And he went everywhere teaching,
healing and preaching." Since teaching is educating
the mind and preaching is educating the heart,
two-thirds of Jesus' work was education.
LAURIE BETH JONES *Jesus, CEO*

GOOD equippers do it like Jesus did it: recruit
twelve, graduate eleven, and focus on three.
LYNN ANDERSON *They Smell Like Sheep*

THE ideal equipper is a person who can impart
the vision of the work, evaluate the potential leader,
give him the tools he needs, and then help him
along the way at the beginning of his journey.
JOHN MAXWELL *Developing the Leaders around You*

GOOD leaders never give their leadership away.
However, they do share both the rewards
and responsibility of leading.
CALVIN MILLER *The Empowered Leader*

SERVANT leaders entrusted with a mission cannot complete that mission on their own. God gives us work to do that is beyond the abilities of a single person, and a leader learns to involve others—their wisdom, gifts, and callings.

When God calls you to service, your job as a leader is to take responsibility for the vision God has imparted. In a sense, you manage the mission. You manage it for the people who are involved with you in the mission, and you manage it for the Lord—the one who gave you the mission in the first place. This is real responsibility!

By its sheer weight and magnitude, the mission forces the leader to share her responsibility with others. In order to accomplish the goal—which goes beyond the abilities and self-interest of the leader—every member of the group must have a sense of responsibility and authority for the task at hand.

How does that happen? Aren't we accustomed to a pastor or other leader presenting a mission or task to a group of believers—and finding that only one or two other people ever catch that vision and come on board? We've seen it happen many, many times. The servant leader ends up being a slave to a task that is way too big for him or her. This isn't the way Jesus worked, and he shows us a better way.

Jesus shared a "BHAG" with his disciples just prior to his ascension to heaven. A BHAG is a "big, hairy audacious goal."[1] Jesus' BHAG for his followers was to make disciples of all nations. Yes, all nations. Jesus was not afraid to share a vision that seemed impossible for his disciples to accomplish on their own. I believe God is in the business of BHAGs! Every great event in God's history with his people began as an audacious goal that seemed impossible until people trusted God and acted on the divine word. From Abraham, who left his home in Ur of the Chaldeans, to Paul, who turned his back on persecuting the church to widening the tent of those in the family of God—men and women of faith have reached impossible goals because they trusted a God with whom nothing is impossible. The commandment Jesus gave his disciples illustrates the God-sized nature of divine mission. Let me rephrase the great commission so you can see how big it really is.

We get our English word *ethnic* from the Greek word translated "nations" in Matthew 28:19. Today we think more in terms of ethnic groups than of nations. We have seen how the nation of Yugoslavia can fall, but the Bosnians and Serbs fight on today. Read the mission as "Go and make disciples of all ethnic groups." This rendering may be more understandable to God's people at the turn of this century than it was to the first disciples. For them, there were only two ethnic groups: Jews and Gentiles. (*Gentiles* is Latin for the same word translated "nations.") Now we know there are over two thousand ethnic groups in the world that have no translation of the Bible. As disciples of Jesus, we share the mission to make disciples of all people groups. That's a kingdom BHAG!

Jesus shared with his disciples the responsibility of bringing God's love to all peoples. That responsibility became their mission. It was huge! Eleven men to make disciples of all ethnic groups?! How was that possible?

HOW DID JESUS DO IT?

HOW did Jesus, as the leader of this eternal mission, empower his team of eleven to carry out this audacious goal of taking his message to all ethnic groups? First, Jesus had already accepted the responsibility of this mission. His death on the cross proved that he accepted the responsibility to reach all people with the love of God. His teachings and actions throughout his life showed his obedience to do his heavenly Father's will. When Jesus called the disciples to himself on the side of a hill and commissioned them to continue that mission, he was not abdicating his own responsibility for it—he was sharing that responsibility. Servant leaders remain responsible for the mission even when they recruit others to complete it.

....

RESPONSIBILITY WITHOUT AUTHORITY
DISABLES RATHER THAN EMPOWERS
FOLLOWERS.

....

Responsibility must be paired with authority.
Jesus, however, did not share only his responsibility; he also shared his authority. *Responsibility without authority disables*

rather than empowers followers. If you say, "Please help by doing thus and so, but don't make any decisions without checking with me," you have not empowered the person; you have enslaved him. Kennon Callahan reminds us that there must be a balance between delegated authority and responsibility. "More authority and fewer responsibilities help persons grow forward in their leadership; less authority and more responsibilities help persons develop passive behavior."[2]

Jesus remained steward of his Father's mission, but he enabled others to carry it out by sharing his authority with them. He did this when he said to his disciples of every generation: "All authority in heaven and on earth has been given to me. Therefore go and make disciples" (Matt. 28:18-19).

"In the name of Jesus . . ."

"In the name of Jesus" is an important phrase throughout the book of Acts and the letters of the apostles. The name of Jesus was the basis of the disciples' authority to stand against earthly powers and governments as they brought the message of Jesus to all people. Peter and John stood boldly before the religious supreme court in Jerusalem and evoked the name of Jesus—not their own authority—as the power behind healing the blind man on the temple steps (Acts 4:10). By using the authority in the name of Jesus, the disciples had the power to carry the Good News to the "ends of the earth" (Acts 1:8). The authority of Jesus allowed them to become "Christ's ambassadors" (2 Cor. 5:20).

We often overlook the fact that Jesus stated his authority to send before he sent his followers on the mission. Leaders who send others without the authority to make decisions send powerless followers to defeat. Where did Jesus' authority come from? It came from his defeat of all powers and principalities through the work of his death, burial, and resurrection. The Son of God was about to take his eternal place above all things. As leader, Jesus claimed his authority to send those he had recruited before sending them out. Jesus shared his authority along with his responsibility to make disciples of all people. This is the foundation for our sixth principle of servant leadership:

> *Servant leaders share their responsibility*
> *and authority to meet a greater need.*

SHARED RESPONSIBILITY AND
AUTHORITY FREE PEOPLE TO GROW

The church in Jerusalem experienced great growth and fellowship through the presence of God's Spirit in people's lives. But as the church grew, an internal cancer threatened to stop the movement of God.

Grumbling was an internal threat
to the growth of the church.

As people came into the church, the number of needs grew. Acts 6:1 tells how the apostles had not met the needs of certain members of the fellowship. People were grumbling. Greek-speaking widows were doing no more than saying, "Hey, you said you would feed us. When the Meals-on-Wheels cart comes by, no one stops at our house. What's up with that?"

....

GRUMBLING BY MEMBERS ON
A MISSION SIMPLY MEANS THAT LEADERS
HAVE NEGLECTED TO ADDRESS
A NEED ADEQUATELY.

....

I used to disregard grumblers. I thought they were a bug in the leader's software. Some days I want to put one of those number dispensers on the door of my office with a sign that reads, "Take a number!" During times of transition and change, grumblers tend to take up most of the leader's time. Remember, too, that some people are naturally grumblers. They are the ones who see the glass as half empty and the sky as partly cloudy. But when someone on mission with you begins to make noises about things not getting done, you had better pay attention. Those team members may see a blind spot you have overlooked.

Grumbling by members on mission simply means that leaders have neglected to address a need adequately. Criticism may be the source of new opportunities. Doug Murren invites us to consider criticism as a gift. He writes, "If we embrace criticism instead of resisting it, we may be presented with new opportunities of service that in turn may open up vistas of success we would have never seen without criticism."[3]

Distributing authority helped the church solve its problems.

The first church did not have enough leaders to oversee the daily distribution of food. The apostles' inability to serve all the members resulted in division and grumbling. To address this need, the leading apostles redefined their role as servants to the Word of God. Their place in the church was to know, preach, and teach the good news of Jesus Christ in order to make disciples. In this way, they were stewards of the vision and core values of the mission. The leaders said they would "give our attention to prayer and the ministry of the word." *Ministry* in this verse is the same word for *servant* that Jesus used when he said that the great ones among his followers must serve others (Mark 10:44).

The church had members with an unmet need. To neglect that need would mean continued division and hurt in the body, but the apostles wisely shared the responsibility of this need with qualified members of the church. They delegated this task to seven members who met the qualifications of being "full of the Spirit and wisdom" (Acts 6:3). The apostles multiplied their leadership by delegating some of their responsibility and authority to others in order to meet the needs of the fellowship.

The apostles delegated their authority to care for the neglected widows. How did the apostles delegate their authority? They "laid their hands on them" (Acts 6:6). This was not the first ordination service. Laying on of hands is a biblical symbol of passing on authority. The Israelites laid their hands on the Levites to give them authority to sacrifice (Num. 8:10). Moses laid his hands on Joshua as a sign that the son of Nun was his successor and that Moses shared the authority God had given him with the new leader (Num. 27:18).

The apostles stood the seven servants in front of the gathered church and placed their hands on them to symbolize the sharing of their authority. They were saying by this act, "These seven have our authority to make decisions related to this issue. What they say goes in regard to the Meals-on-Wheels routes in the Greek-speaking neighborhoods." Note that the apostles gave no instructions as to how they were to meet the need. Genuine delegation leaves the details to those entrusted with their part of the mission.

The next phrase in Acts is "so the word of God spread" (Acts 6:7). Why? Delegated authority and responsibility allowed needs to be met and empowered others to carry out the mission of the church. Calvin Miller observes, "Good leaders never give their leadership away. However, they do share both the rewards and responsibilities of leadership."[4] The apostles delegated enough authority for the seven to make decisions to meet the people's needs and so did not frustrate those they asked to help.

EQUIP OTHERS TO SHARE
RESPONSIBILITY AND AUTHORITY

Paul reminded the church in Ephesus: "It was he [Christ] who gave some to be apostles, some to be prophets, some to be evangelists, and some to be pastors and teachers, to prepare God's people for works of service, so that the body of Christ may be built up" (Eph. 4:11-12). In essence, the Bible teaches that God places his gifts in the church with specifically gifted people who can prepare others for service and thus further the church's mission. The word translated "to prepare" can also be translated "to equip" (NASB). So we see that not only does a servant leader recruit others for the mission, he actually equips those people so that they will be effective servants of God.

"To equip" gets its meaning from two different contexts in New Testament times. One was the medical world. To equip meant to set a broken bone in order to prepare it for healing. In that context, it meant "to put in order."[5] The second context was the fishing industry. Fishermen would "equip" their nets at the end of a casting period. They would restore the net to its former condition and allow the sun to dry it in its designed position. In this way they prepared the net for casting.

These two pictures provide leaders with images of their job. To equip the church is to prepare its members to perform their part of the mission. If the church were a net, the leader's job would be to prepare that net for its next cast. He would do this by making sure each person is in her proper place according to the design of the net and in right relationship with the rest of the net. The biblical picture of the church is a body. The leader's job in this image may be to set fractured parts of the body so they can heal and eventually function as part of the whole body.

Our staff went away for its quarterly meeting one year and sought to define why we did what we did. After brainstorming, some wordsmithing, and voting multiple times, we came up with the following mission statement: The staff exists to equip people to carry out the mission of Legacy Drive Baptist Church by building relationships and modeling servant leadership.

We agreed that God set people aside for part-time and full-time service to equip people for ministry, not to do that ministry by themselves. After we completed our work, someone noted that the statement was nothing more than Ephesians 4:11-12. He was right! Once again, we had stumbled onto a path God had intended from the beginning. God gifts the church with leaders not to do ministry alone but to equip members of the body to do ministry. The ministry of the staff is to equip others. I tell my directors of ministries: "It is your responsibility not to do the job but to see that the job gets done."

HOW TO EQUIP
OTHERS FOR SERVICE

IF YOU are a leader, you will serve those you lead by equipping them to do their part in God's plan. I would like to suggest five steps to equip others:[6]

- ❖ Encourage them to serve;
- ❖ Qualify them to serve;
- ❖ Understand their needs;
- ❖ Instruct them; and
- ❖ Pray for them.

These five steps will allow you to share your responsibility and authority as a leader.

ENCOURAGE THEM

Jesus called the Twelve to follow him to the cross and to be his witnesses to the ends of the earth. He spent much of his time with his disciples, encouraging them. John 14 contains some of Jesus' most encouraging words to his followers. His disciples were concerned for themselves and their master. The closer they came to Jerusalem, the more troubled they became about what would happen to them and to Jesus. Jesus turned to his followers and said, "Do not let your hearts be troubled." He saw their fear and addressed it. He didn't chastise them for being worried! If you want to lead people as Jesus led, be aware of their struggles and fears—and make a point to encourage them in the midst of those things.

One of my favorite New Testament characters is Barnabas. His real name was Joseph. Barnabas, his nickname, means "Son of Encouragement" (Acts 4:36). I don't know how God would have brought Saul of Tarsus into the ethnic mission without Barnabas. This leader in the Jerusalem church was the first to encourage the church to accept the newly converted Saul. He did this by putting his arm around Saul and saying, "I know this guy. He's the real thing. I know he used to persecute the church, but the Head of the church has commissioned him to be on the mission with us. You can trust him" (see Acts 9:27).

Later, when Barnabas saw what God was doing in Antioch, he traveled to Tarsus and encouraged Saul to come with him and teach the Scriptures to the new believers. The Bible says that after a year of teaching and ministering to those God was gathering to be the church in the mission outpost of Antioch, "the disciples were called Christians first at Antioch" (Acts 11:26). Barnabas encouraged Paul to join him in ministry. That ultimately led to the church's setting these two aside to begin the work of carrying the gospel around the world.

I have had several men like Barnabas in my life. These were men who came up to me, put an arm around me, and said, "I think you can do this." I remember sending a manuscript to Calvin Miller and asking for his input on it. The concept was a series of devotional thoughts called *Altars in the Sand*. Calvin wrote me an incredibly encouraging letter, but he was honest enough to say, "Don't quit your day job! This thing needs some work." Although he basically said, "You're not ready yet," he kindly encouraged me to keep working on my writing. Others have encouraged me to complete my studies and to pastor. Church members who have encouraged me to lead have motivated me to take risks I normally would not take. These people—all of whom I have nicknamed Barnabas—along with my parents and wife have encouraged me to live out God's call on my life.

You probably have a Barnabas in your life too. Take a moment to remember the power of that person's words when he or she said, "You can do this." One of the greatest acts of a servant leader is to be a Barnabas to another person.

QUALIFY THEM

To encourage someone to become involved in ministry is not enough. Encouragement without training is like enthusiasm without direction: You move around a lot, but little gets done!

SERVANT LEADERS QUALIFY THOSE THEY ENCOURAGE TO JOIN THEM ON MISSION. Qualifying for mission includes meeting certain expectations related to being a follower of Christ. These expectations include the person's spiritual condition—is he fit for the place in which you have encouraged him to serve?

Jesus qualified those who followed him by holding up high standards of discipleship. Luke tells us that after Jesus told the story about taking the backseat at the banquet, "large crowds were traveling with Jesus" (Luke 14:25). Most church leaders would see this as a good thing and would report it to their state papers! Jesus, on the other hand, knew that most of those following had no clue what following him actually meant. Jesus turned to the crowd and said, "If anyone comes to me and does not hate his father and mother, his wife and children, his brothers and sisters—yes, even his own life—he cannot be my disciple" (Luke 14:26). Not a consumer-driven invitation, was it? Jesus wanted to qualify those who followed him by holding up standards of discipleship. He wanted everyone who bought into the mission to understand its cost.

Jesus was very clear about the cost of discipleship. He risked losing large numbers of followers in order to keep those who trusted him and his mission. As a leader who follows Jesus' example, you should make the cost of service very clear to those you encourage to join you.

....

THE DANGER OF LEGALISM EXISTS ANYTIME YOU HOLD A PERSON UP TO BIBLICAL STANDARDS OF DISCIPLESHIP.
....

A word of caution. You can expect too much of a person before he is more mature in Christ. The danger of legalism exists anytime you hold a person up to biblical standards of discipleship. No one lives up to the biblical ideal. You are a minister "not of the letter but of the Spirit; for the letter kills, but the Spirit gives life" (2 Cor. 3:6). The opposite danger of legalism, however, is to have no standards for those who serve in the church. Too many churches suffer because those recruited to serve on mission are not biblically qualified to serve. Servant leaders seek a loving balance between biblical standards and the reality of human sinfulness.

....

TOO MANY CHURCHES SUFFER BECAUSE THOSE RECRUITED TO SERVE ON MISSIONS ARE NOT BIBLICALLY QUALIFIED TO SERVE.
....

A SERVANT LEADER QUALIFIES THOSE HE EQUIPS BY KNOWING THEIR SKILLS AND GIFTEDNESS RELATED TO THE MINISTRY HE HAS ASKED THEM TO DO. The leader must know whether or not a person is competent for a particular ministry. A leader must ask the questions, "Does this person understand how what I have asked her to do relates to the mission?" "Does this person know how to do what I am asking her to do?" The Bible provides a model for qualifying others for service in this sense.

Paul gave Timothy what I call the "2-2-2 Plan for Discipleship" from 2 Timothy 2:2. The pattern of sharing the message of Jesus as outlined by Paul was

Paul ⟶ Timothy ⟶ reliable men ⟶ others

Paul was Timothy's mentor. Paul equipped Timothy as they traveled together (Acts 16:1-5). When Paul felt Timothy was qualified to do ministry without him, he left Timothy in Ephesus to lead the church (1 Tim. 1:3). Paul later wrote to the young pastor and told him to entrust what he learned from Paul to faithful men who would also "be qualified to teach others" (2 Tim. 2:2). "Qualified" in this verse means to be fit or competent for something. Paul told Timothy to find "reliable," or faithful, men whom he could train to teach others. That pattern is still valid for equipping leaders today. A contemporary model of Paul's instructions would be:

your mentor ⟶ you ⟶ faithful members ⟶ others

Servant leaders qualify those they encourage to join them on mission so that those they qualify can pass the mission on to others.

UNDERSTAND THEIR NEEDS

Jesus equipped his disciples by understanding their needs. He did this in at least two ways. When he came off the Mount of Trans-figuration, a man brought his sick boy to Jesus. He made the point that he had already brought his son to Jesus' disciples, and they could do nothing to help. Jesus healed the boy. Later, the disciples asked Jesus why they were unable to heal the man's son. Jesus made the observation, "This kind can come out only by prayer" (Mark 9:29). Jesus had observed his followers and seen that they made too little time for the disciplines that produce power in one's spiritual life. Jesus understood their need for spiritual disciplines by observing the lack of power in their ministry.

Another time, the disciples came to Jesus with a request. After watching Jesus pray all night and seeing the power of God in his life, the disciples asked Jesus to teach them to pray (Luke 11:1-4). Jesus responded by teaching them the Disciple's Prayer. Jesus understood their need because he listened to their request. He equipped the Twelve for ministry by modeling prayer in front of them and responding to their request when they asked him about this habit in his life.

How does Jesus' example apply to your role as someone who must equip others? To understand the needs of those you are responsible for, observe them in ministry and listen to their requests.

To observe a team member in ministry is to discover what he needs in order to complete the task. Coaches make good use of observation. They spend hours between games reviewing and analyzing films to see how the team performed. To prepare for the next game, they design practices around what they saw on the films. Leaders observe those they have recruited in order to evaluate their performance and to understand what is lacking in their skills and resources. When was the last time you sat in a room with a teacher or completed an observation report on someone you are responsible for? If we don't observe the people we're leading, and if we're not honest about what they lack and therefore need, we may as well bury our heads in the sand and forget about accomplishing any mission.

Listening is the easiest way to understand the needs of people who are in ministry with you. You don't need complicated report forms and status reports to know what others need to complete their task. Simply ask the question, "What do you need to do your job?" Then listen.

Listening is a discipline. Leaders who are goal oriented miss opportunities to serve when they forget to listen to those they are leading. Listening is time-consuming but essential to a leader's success. Listening is hard work, but it leads to opportunities to serve those whom you have recruited.

I am naturally task oriented. Give me a choice between going to a party and checking a project off my list, and I will choose the project. Awhile back, a staff member said we were not growing together as a staff. My first emotional response was defensive. I wanted to blurt out, "We aren't fighting or anything! I could tell you of much worse staff situations." I, however, am ultimately responsible for the staff's well-being, and one of those on my team was raising a concern. As I listened to his concerns and we began to address the problem rather than explain it away, we planned a great time of fellowship that resulted in genuine relationship building and some fun memories. While I preferred not to hear this staff member, listening to him resulted in meeting a need among those I had recruited to carry out the mission of our church.

INSTRUCT THEM

Leaders make a big mistake when they forget to instruct the people they are equipping. Too many times, leaders invite others to become involved in ministry and then leave them alone to guess what they should do. Problems always surface when workers go untrained. Instruction is part of leadership, and it is the fourth step of equipping.

Jesus constantly taught his disciples. He trained them about the nature of the kingdom of God (Matt. 13). He explained his mission (Mark 10:32-34). He performed miracles to teach lessons (Mark 4:35-41). Jesus even instructed his disciples on their attitude about being his followers (Luke 17:7-10).

Paul, the leader who built a worldwide web of churches, also instructed those who were in the ministry with him (see 1 Thess. 4:1-12). The clearest example of this practice is in Paul's letters to Timothy. This young man joined Paul on his second journey to evangelize the ethnics (Acts 16:1-3). Paul left him in Ephesus to lead the church there. Later, Paul wrote to Timothy and explained how he wanted the young leader to serve those he had been entrusted with to make disciples.

First Timothy 4:11-16 is a list of instructions Paul gave his young recruit. Paul instructed Timothy to teach the things he had outlined for him. He told the young man not to let others look down on him because he was young. Paul encouraged him to set an example for others to follow in every area of his life. Paul instructed the young pastor to devote himself to the public reading of Scripture, to preaching and teaching. Paul told him not to neglect his spiritual gift. The senior missionary taught Timothy to be diligent in these matters so that others could see his progress. Finally, Paul instructed Timothy to watch his life and his doctrine closely because others depended on him.

Paul equipped Timothy by teaching him how to minister to those in his care. His instructions were clear and specific. Paul's recruit did not have to wonder what his mentor expected of him. Servant leaders equip others by instructing them in the specific tasks they have been called to do.

····························
THOSE WHO FOLLOW NEED TO KNOW WHERE THEY ARE GOING AND WHAT IS EXPECTED OF THEM.
····························

Those who follow need to know where they are going and what is expected of them. A member of our church described the need for our people to know what's going on: "Our people are like players on the sideline waiting to get into the game. They are motivated and most of them are trained to contribute to the game. They are just waiting for someone to tell them the game plan and their part in it and send them into the game. Most of our church is like a sidelined team waiting to be sent in to play by the coach. If they don't know the game plan or their part in it, they will either become bitter at the coach for not playing them or—in many cases—go look for another team to play on." This is one of several reasons why we have worked hard to establish ways for people to become involved in ministry and find a place to belong in the church.

PRAY FOR THEM

Up to this point, each step to equip others can be done in human strength. You can encourage others under your own power. Your motivation to involve others can simply be because you need help. You can qualify others by your own efforts and standards. You can understand the needs of those you recruit by watching and listening to them. You can even instruct them in attitudes and specifics of their ministry based upon human decisions and understanding. But one thing might still be lacking, even with all these other things in place. *Do the people in your care have God's power in their lives?*

Jesus observed a lack of power in his disciples when they could not cast out a demon (Matt. 17:19-21). Power was the missing, crucial element. Thus, the most important step in equipping others is to pray for them.

....

DO THE PEOPLE IN YOUR CARE HAVE GOD'S POWER IN THEIR LIVES?

....

Jesus made this step a priority in his ministry to his followers. In his final hours with those he loved, he prayed for them. John 17:6-19 is the content of that prayer. In it, he prayed for their unity (v. 11). He prayed that they would have joy in ministry (v. 13). Jesus prayed for their protection (v. 15). He prayed that they remain holy, set apart, by the truth of God's Word (v. 17). Jesus equipped his disciples by praying for them.

Servant leaders pray for those they equip for mission. This is the unique nature of *Christian* leadership. Leaders in the church know that their power comes from God, not themselves. They also know that they are most effective when others support them in prayer. Leaders on mission with Christ are helpless without the prayers of others. These prayers may be all that keeps them standing in times of struggle and conflict.

Jan prays for me and our church. She is part of a group of prayer warriors who seek God and his purposes for our church. They intercede for me and the members of our fellowship. Before there were buildings on our property, Jan would sit in her car and pray over the land. She meets with me every Sunday morning in my office for prayer. We pray for the worship services and those who will teach, lead, and work that day. Jan often leaves me a written prayer with Scripture references for the day. I do not know how I could minister without people like Jan praying for me.

I am convinced that *no servant leader should stand to lead until he kneels to pray with those he serves.* The power of equipping others is not in technique but in prayer. Prayer should permeate every step to equip others. Prayer gives discernment, protection, and power to those who lead. Prayer is God's answer to our weakness as leaders.

In the fall of 1996, our church entered 100 Days of Prayer. After we had settled the issue of leadership earlier in the year, we needed direction. We asked the church members to pray for one hundred consecutive days and simply ask God: "How do you, O God, want to use us?" I began that season of prayer expecting God to reveal himself to someone else first. But just two weeks into the time of prayer, God began to reveal the deep meaning of faith to me.

....

NO SERVANT LEADER SHOULD STAND
TO LEAD UNTIL HE KNEELS TO PRAY
WITH THOSE HE SERVES.

....

God used a meeting with Tom Wolfe, then pastor of Church on Brady in Los Angeles, to show me how God was still completing his mission to reach all people even in my mission field. God used a sermon tape by Bruce Wilkerson, the founder of Walk Through the Bible, to teach me the faithful prayer of Jabez. God used a royalty check and a member's confession of God's provision in his business to teach me how to use tangible assets to make intangible realities come into being.

At the end of those one hundred days, we knew our theme and our goals for the next year. God had said, "It's harvesttime!" (Matt. 9:35-38). In response to that call, we would expand the number of laborers in the field through witness and ministry training. We would expand the number of ministries in the field by adding one new ministry a month to reach those in our community. We would expand the number of staff to equip our people for the harvest, and we would expand our facilities to provide space for the harvest God would pour out on our church. We are in the process of reaching every one of those goals in tangible, measurable ways.

We are in another 100 Days of Prayer as I write this paragraph. We have begun again to sense God's leadership to continue our preparation and acceptance of his harvest call on our church. As we come into 1998, God is giving us the focus and direction for our church. How? One word: *prayer.*

....

YOU SERVE BECAUSE YOU HAVE BEEN
CALLED, NOT BECAUSE YOU DECIDED TO
MAKE THE WORLD A BETTER PLACE.

....

Let me also say a word about the need for prayer in the leader's life. Jesus was a leader who prayed. Why? I am convinced that those hours in prayer with his Father were first of all times of worship and glory of his Father. Worship is the nuclear reactor of a servant leader's passion. Without a vital relationship with the One who called you to mission, you will lose your passion to serve. *You serve because you have been called, not because you decided to make the world a better place.* Worship is the energy source for passion in a servant leader's life.

I also believe Jesus spent time in prayer to receive direction and clarity for his mission. Once Jesus became servant to his Father's mission, he had to spend time making sure he was on God's mission, not his own. Prayer and fasting focused his mission and aided him to overcome the temptation of shortcuts to the kingdom. In prayer, Jesus learned who to choose for his leadership team. In prayer, God confirmed his call on Jesus' life at the Transfiguration. In prayer, Jesus laid down his will for the will of his Father. Jesus carried out the Father's call on his life through the power of prayer.

Leaders who are servants to God's mission will spend time in prayer with the One who called them and who empowers them. Prayer is the source of vision, direction, correction, and resources for mission. Servants to the mission must stay on-line with their Master in order to complete that mission. Prayer is the greatest source of strength for the servant leader.

These are not the only five things you can do to equip others. To equip someone means spending time with him. It means knowing the one you are equipping well enough to customize how you do the equipping. John Maxwell reminds us that equipping, like nurturing, is an ongoing process. You don't equip with formulas or videotapes, he writes.

> Equipping must be tailored to each potential leader. . . .
> The ideal equipper is a person who can impart the vision of the work, evaluate the potential leader, give him the tools he needs, and then help him along the way at the beginning of his journey.[7]

SHARE RESPONSIBILITY AND AUTHORITY IN THE HOME AND MARKETPLACE

The principle of sharing responsibility and authority applies to relationships in the home and in the marketplace. Here are two examples.

Principle #6 in the home
William Mitchell, author of *Power of Positive Parents* and *Building Strong Families,* claims that every parent is a leader.

Dr. Mitchell believes that "leadership within a family structure is very likely a matter of steering a child's negative impulses into a positive expression."[8] The sixth principle of sincerely servant leadership reinforces the following comments by Dr. Mitchell:

> The concepts of authority and responsibility go hand in hand. The more your child assumes responsibility for his own life, the more authority he should have over his life. But until your child bears the *full* responsibility for his behavior before God and society, the parent is in authority over that child.[9]

Part of parenting is sharing responsibility and authority with children so they can live out God's plan for their lives.

I was in youth ministry for eleven years before becoming a pastor. I am now the father of a teenager. You can spot a child whose parents have shared both authority and responsibility with a teen. Those parents who shared only the responsibility of family and school produced very dependent children. Dependency is not bad in a four-year-old, but by fourteen, a child should have authority to make some decisions in her life. On the other hand, those parents who gave their teens the authority of an adult soon discovered that their child could not handle the responsibilities of life. In a teen, total freedom to choose does not guarantee responsibility in an adult.

Principle #6 in the marketplace

How do you translate this principle into your calling in the marketplace? As a servant leader, you should be about equipping those who have been entrusted to you to carry out the mission of your company or organization. Here are some practical suggestions based on our study of Jesus.

❖ Encourage those on your team to join you on mission.

❖ Make the effort to "put your arm around them" through notes and gifts.

❖ Look for people with potential, and invite them to take leadership positions.

❖ Go out of your way to celebrate successes among those who follow you.

❖ Qualify those you recruit and those who are entrusted to you.

❖ If you are a leader in a church or religious organization, qualify the heart of those you are equipping by hearing about their spiritual journey and testing their spiritual maturity.

❖ Make sure you have mission statements for each responsibility you share with others. This will keep you from sharing authority to carry out an unclear responsibility.

❖ Know the person's S.E.R.V.E. profile, and check to see if she matches the needs of the task she's been given.

❖ Understand the needs of those on mission with you.

❖ Take time to observe those on mission with you in the task you have assigned to them.

❖ Spend all the time and energy needed to listen to those you have recruited. They will give you a list of needs and "to dos" that will allow you to serve them.

❖ Create an atmosphere of honesty and openness so that those who follow will feel free to share their needs with you.

❖ Instruct each member of your team in the task you have assigned to her. Give clear instructions about the tasks you expect to see accomplished.

❖ Check each member's attitudes toward you and your instructions. This will indicate whether or not you have communicated clearly and whether or not you have shared enough authority to accomplish the assigned task.

❖ Keep a record of meetings and messages in order to track your effectiveness in instruction.

❖ Pray for those on your team.

❖ Pray for each person you are equipping. Even in a secular setting, it is appropriate to tell a coworker or employee you are praying for her. I have never had anyone resist this statement. At the very least, you will get the response, "Thanks. I need all the help I can get."

❖ If you are a leader in a church or religious organization, take time to pray with each person for whom you are responsible. Listen to his needs and pause to pray with him.

❖ As the leader, spend extended time in prayer and quiet waiting. God can use this time to give you direction and insight into situations you face. God can also keep you on your divine mission while carrying out the company's mission.

This principle of servant leadership will empower you to lead those you have recruited to join you in Christ's mission. Servant leaders equip. What else do they do? The next principle answers that question.

FOR STUDY AND REFLECTION

- What responsibility did Jesus share with his disciples? Do you consider this a responsibility for you as a servant leader? If so, how do you articulate this responsibility for those around you?

- How did Jesus share his authority with his disciples? How can you use that same authority in your ministry to others?

- List the five steps to equip those on mission with you. E_____
  Q_____ U_____ I_____ P_____.

- Who is a Barnabas in your life, the person who encouraged you to become involved in service? Write his or her name and what he or she encouraged you to do.

- List two ways you can understand the needs of those you are equipping for ministry.

- What are your feelings about the role of prayer in a leader's life? Write out your personal belief about prayer and the role it plays in your personal life. Are you praying for someone? Do you have someone to pray for you?

- If you are a parent, how can you share responsibility and authority with your children? List one or two examples for each child.

- Summarize principle 6 in your own words. List three ways you can apply this principle in your life this week.

Endnotes for Principle #6

1. James C. Collins and Jerry I. Porras, *Built to Last* (New York: Harper Business, 1997), 91–114. Collins and Porras have demonstrated that these kinds of goals are one of the habits of successful, visionary companies in American business.

2. Kennon Callahan, *Effective Church Leadership* (New York: Harper & Row, 1990), 157.

3. Doug Murren, *Leadershift* (Ventura, Calif.: Regal, 1994), 157.

4. Calvin Miller, *The Empowered Leader* (Nashville: Broadman & Holman, 1995), 158.

5. Arndt and Gingrich, 419.

6. C. Gene Wilkes, *Jesus on Leadership* (Nashville: LifeWay Press, 1990), 85–102.

7. John Maxwell, *Developing the Leaders around You* (Nashville: Nelson, 1995), 84.

8. William Mitchell and Michael A. Mitchell, *Building Strong Families* (Nashville: Broadman & Holman, 1997), 30.

9. Ibid., 35.

BUILD A TEAM

THERE is no success without a successor.
JOHN MAXWELL *Developing the Leaders around You*

IN ORDER to build a true team spirit, you must
delegate accountability and glory as well as
responsibility.
CALVIN MILLER *The Empowered Leader*

BASIC changes take place very slowly, if at all, because
those with the power generally have no knowledge,
and those with the knowledge have no power.
WARREN BENNIS *Why Leaders Can't Lead*

GOOD spiritual leaders are shepherds, not saviors,
leaders not lords, guides not gods.
LYNN ANDERSON *They Smell Like Sheep*

JANET leads a ministry team. This team began when Janet stepped forward to invest her vocational skill of teaching English as a second language to make disciples through the ministry of our church. She told me one day that she taught ESL at the local community college and felt she wanted to present the gospel to her students. She asked if we could offer classes at the church and use the Bible as the student textbook. Our church had begun to talk about how we needed to see our community as a mission field and how we needed to "do foreign missions at home." Teaching English with the Bible as the primary text was a proven method of teaching people language and the love of God! While we had never considered ministry to internationals as part of our vision, God called Janet to lead us into this vital ministry.

Janet started this ministry alone. In four years, however, she has equipped and empowered a team of seventeen people to serve over two hundred internationals connected to our church.[1] This ministry team has served our church's mission by providing international families with three opportunities per week to be involved in language instruction and study of the Bible as a primary textbook. Our English as a second language ministry has also distributed over two hundred Bibles in ten different languages free of charge to those enrolled in the ministry. Janet and her ESL team are a model of team ministry.

THE TEAM JESUS BUILT

A LEADER is more like a player on a soccer team than like a pro golfer on tour. Golfers need to motivate and train only themselves. As a matter of fact, golfers in competition sort of enjoy watching the other guy lose it on the last hole to blow the match—if they don't do the same! A team player, on the other hand, must make sure not only that she is motivated, is trained, and has the right attitude but that everyone on the team has the same interest and willingness to accomplish the goal. Team leaders have more than just themselves to care for.

....

YOU WILL NEVER BE AN EFFECTIVE LEADER UNTIL YOU INCLUDE THOSE YOU LEAD IN WHAT YOU DO.

....

Leaders must involve others to reach a shared goal, and they fail when they put too much trust in their own efforts and those efforts alone. You will never be an effective leader until you include those you lead in what you do. Trust me. I have discovered just how true this is. Leaders go nowhere until they involve followers in making decisions and planning how goals will be reached. You cannot lead unless others are just as moved by the vision and sense of mission as you are. And it's up to you to create that vision/mission and bring those you lead into it with you.

The goal of this book is to cultivate servant leaders in team ministry. Servant leaders flourish with ministry teams. These teams are how leaders do their best work. Teams are superior to individual effort for several reasons:

- ❖ Teams involve more people, thus affording more resources, ideas, and energy than would an individual.

- ❖ Teams maximize a leader's potential and minimize her weaknesses. Strengths and weaknesses are more exposed in individuals.

- ❖ Teams provide multiple perspectives of how to meet a need or reach a goal, thus devising several alternatives for each situation. Individual insight is seldom as broad and deep as a group's when it takes on a problem.

- ❖ Teams share the credit for victories and the blame for losses. This fosters genuine humility and authentic community. Individuals take credit and blame alone. This fosters pride and sometimes a sense of failure.

- ❖ Teams keep leaders accountable for the goal. Individuals connected to no one can change the goal without accountability.

- ❖ Teams can simply do more than an individual.

- ❖ Teams are how Jesus did ministry.

WHY DID JESUS NEED THE DISCIPLES?

If we are born again through Jesus alone, why did he invest so much love, time, and energy in his disciples? Jesus came to carry out his Father's mission. He stated it: "The Son of Man [came] . . . to give his life as a ransom for many" (Mark 10:45). He accomplished his mission on earth when he died, was buried, and was raised on the third day.

So, what were the disciples about? Why couldn't Jesus have just come, lived and taught, died and been raised, gone back to heaven, and waited for people to trust him?

Jesus' ministry on earth is a striking example of an important leadership principle: Mission continues when people are captured by it, equipped to do it, and "teamed" to carry it on. When Jesus turned his motley crew of disciples into a team with a mission, he ensured that his work would continue long after he was gone. If only we could truly grasp what this means. God intended all along for people to participate with him in the eternal mission to bring people into the kingdom. Even his own Son's incarnation and carrying out of this mission wasn't enough. Jesus modeled God's intention for people like you and me so that we could be connected to his mission.

....

GOD INTENDED ALL ALONG FOR PEOPLE
TO PARTICIPATE WITH HIM IN THE
ETERNAL MISSION TO BRING PEOPLE
INTO THE KINGDOM.

....

Jesus seldom did ministry by himself. Jesus was Lord and Master and needed no one to help him. Yet no matter what he was doing, he ministered with his disciples nearby. He usually had at least three disciples with him wherever he went. By constantly having his closest followers near him, he showed how the best lessons came from the classroom of experience. In the sense that Jesus was all-powerful and could do whatever he wanted, he did not need a ministry team, but he built one so that his mission would continue when he returned to the Father.

Mark 6:7 is a description of how Jesus built a ministry team: "Calling the Twelve to him, he sent them out two by two and gave them authority over evil spirits." This description is the basis of our seventh principle of servant leadership:

Servant leaders multiply their leadership by empowering others to lead.

Mark 6:7 provides the elements for this principle.

"CALLING THE TWELVE." Jesus called the disciples to carry out his mission to reach the lost and establish his kingdom on earth. Servant leadership begins with a call to be servant to the mission of God.

"TO HIM." This phrase describes Jesus' role as the leader. Leaders invite others to join them on mission.

"HE SENT THEM OUT TWO BY TWO." This tells us that Jesus was willing to multiply his leadership in others. Teams of at least two followers were part of his strategy for this. Jesus demonstrated that implementing a mission is not an individual effort. Teams are the best vehicle by which to do God's work.

"[HE] GAVE THEM AUTHORITY OVER EVIL SPIRITS." Jesus empowered those he called. We will see later how Jesus modeled empowerment for his followers.

Jesus called twelve followers to himself to carry out his mission with him. He sent them out in teams of two to try their hand at ministering to a lost world. Jesus empowered his disciples with his own authority to overcome opposition and do the work of the kingdom. Jesus modeled team ministry to illustrate that until he returns, his mission to bring the kingdom of God on earth is best accomplished by servant leaders in team ministry.

WHY TEAM?

A team is a group of people bound together by a commitment to reach a shared goal. A team can be a group of college students playing intramural football. It can be a group of researchers seeking the cure for a disease. A group of Sunday school workers teaching the Bible to a roomful of four-year-olds can be a team, too. A team can put a space probe on Mars or feed the poor.

Business has recognized the power of teams. The Harvard business school says that a team is

> a small number of people with complementary skills who are committed to a common purpose, performance goals, and approach for which they hold themselves mutually accountable.[2]

These authors claim that high-performance teams should be the basic unit of performance for most organizations, regardless of size.[3]

Leaders build teams to multiply their influence. John Maxwell has demonstrated that a leader's highest return is "forming a dream team of leaders."[4] According to Greenleaf, the leader in a group of leaders is "whoever in the council has the greatest team-building ability."[5] Building teams is a core value for successful leadership in any organization or movement.

A committee is not a team!

Be sure you understand one crucial distinction: Committees and teams are different. Committees belong to an institutional structure and mind-set. They protect and guide the institution.

Committees are groups of people who meet and make decisions for others. Agendas and meetings are everything to committees.

....

COMMITTEES CONTROL.
BUT TEAMS EMPOWER.

....

Teams, on the other hand, fit inside the structure and mind-set of a mission; they live not for an institution but for the purpose of reaching that mission goal. Teams don't make decisions for everyone else. Their decisions are for themselves only and are related directly to the task at hand. To a team, mission-related goals are everything. *Committees control. But teams empower.*

Let's go back to Janet's desire to start teaching English as a second language in our church. In a committee-driven culture, she would have drawn up a proposal and probably attended meetings of at least the trustees, finance committee, and building-use committee. Since committees exist to make decisions for others, Janet could have spent many months answering questions related to money, meeting rooms, and legal issues. Janet could still be teaching her ESL classes in the community college by herself!

In a team-driven culture like our church, I simply gave Janet permission to gather a leadership team and offer classes. The staff directors and I guided the process of development until Janet had the ministry running on its own. We informed the finance and facility teams along the way, and they advised on money and space issues as the ministry grew. I meet monthly with Janet to pray for her and the ministry and to be a resource for her and the international families she reaches with her team. In our church, teams exist to do ministry, not make decisions for others. I am so pleased we don't have committees.

In light of all this, what is a team ministry—as opposed to a committee or some other organization? Here's my working definition: Team ministry is a group of disciples, bound together under the lordship of Christ, who are committed to the shared goal of meeting a particular need related to the overall mission of the church.

Ministry teams are different from teams in the marketplace in some key ways. The glue of ministry teams is the shared work of Christ in each member of the team. The lordship of the Servant Leader in each member's life ensures a common set of core values and goals. Each member shares a similar sense of calling by God on his life. The goal of ministry teams is to meet needs in order to more effectively carry out Christ's mission in the world. This is the servant side of teams formed within the church. Servant teams do set goals and hold one another accountable for reaching those goals. But the focus is on serving others rather than increasing the bottom line.

Leadership of a team is the highest expression of servant leadership.

This is true because team leadership embodies each of the principles of servant leadership:

- ❖ You must humble yourself in order to build a team (principle 1). Humility allows you to see the need for others. Pride insists on working alone.

- ❖ You cannot seek a position and have the team succeed (principle 2). Following Jesus keeps you on mission and out of competition with others.

- ❖ You must be willing to give up your personal right to be served and find greatness in service to the mission and the other team members (principle 3).

❖ You must trust that God is in control of your life in order to risk service to those on the team (principle 4).

❖ You must take up the towel of service to meet the needs of the group (principle 5).

❖ You must share both responsibility and authority with team members in order to meet the greater need of the team's goal (principle 6).

❖ You must multiply your leadership by empowering other members of the team to lead (principle 7).

❖ Team ministry is how servant leaders do the work of mission. In our servant leadership model we see that team is how the leader best serves those he has recruited for mission.

Our goal in this final chapter is to give you four steps to build your ministry team.

HOW DOES A SERVANT LEADER BUILD A TEAM?

BUILDING a team involves these four steps:

- ❖ Create a sense of togetherness;
- ❖ Empower with authority and presence;
- ❖ Account for the mission and the team's actions;
- ❖ Be a mentor.[6]

CREATE A SENSE OF TOGETHERNESS

Team ministry begins when there is a sense of being part of something important. The first characteristic of a team is that "we are in this together." Effective teams work because members sense that each person belongs, that they share a common goal and have a purpose for functioning. Team ministry can start when those on the team sense that they are together for a reason greater than themselves.

Bill Mitchell is the founder of Power of Positive Parenting.[7] He began building a similar program, Power of Positive Students, while he was the superintendent of a South Carolina school system.

His goal: Help students and teachers believe in themselves. The success of the program led to helping parents instill self-confidence in their children. My favorite saying from Bill came from when he was a high school coach in Alabama. Coach Bill wanted to instill a sense of unity and to ensure that no one player thought himself more important than the others. So every player had a phrase printed on his T-shirt under his uniform: "Big Team, Little Me." This slogan said that every player was a part of the larger team, but no player found importance in himself above the others. "Big Team, Little Me" built a sense of togetherness on Coach Mitchell's teams. That sense of being part of something bigger than yourself can build a sense of unity among your team members.

How do you know if team members have a sense that they are "in this together"? Here are four truths that point to a team's sense of togetherness.

Team ministry means that every member has a place on the team.

Each member helps move the team toward its goal through his or her unique contribution to the team. Different spiritual gifts, experiences, relational styles, vocational skills, and enthusiasm make a ministry team complete. Diversity is a good thing in team ministry. Peter Drucker has noted:

> A common mistake is to believe that because individuals are all on the same team, they all think alike and act alike. Not so. The purpose of a team is to make the strengths of each person effective, and his or her weaknesses irrelevant.[8]

Stephen Covey puts it this way: "The role of the leader is to foster mutual respect and build a complementary team where each strength is made productive and each weakness made irrelevant."[9] Putting a team together means finding people who share a common goal with you but who may act and think differently from you. Team ministry reinforces the biblical teaching that the church is many parts but one body.

This is why knowing a team member's S.E.R.V.E. profile is important. If you are building the team, you want people whose spiritual gifts, relational styles, and vocational skills are different from yours. If your spiritual gift is teaching, for example, you will want someone on the team with the gift of exhortation to encourage you to move beyond analysis to action. If your relational style is "steadiness," you will want someone with a relational style of "dominance" on your team to help you make decisions. If you lack certain vocational skills necessary to meet the need, invite someone on the team who has those skills and shares your passion to meet that need. Unity in diversity is the biblical model for togetherness (1 Cor. 12:12). Every member belongs.

Teams form to reach a common goal—a goal related to the overall mission of the organization.

It is essential to successful ministry that there be unity around the ministry's goals. The goals themselves should help create a sense of togetherness. It is the leader's responsibility to build this sense of unity through a continual articulation of the goal.

Jesus insisted that those who followed him share his values and purposes. He said, "He who is not with me is against me, and he who does not gather with me scatters" (Matt. 12:30). Jesus made sure that anyone wanting to be on his team shared his mission. A team that is together "gathers." A team in disunity "scatters."

The seven principles of servant leadership can become the shared goals of a marriage. These behavioral goals become the standard of how spouses act toward one another. I have written the principles of servant leadership as core values for my marriage this way:

❖ We will humble ourselves before God and toward each other.

❖ We will follow Jesus first, pursue careers second.

❖ We will give up our rights to be served and find greatness in service to each other.

❖ We will risk everything earthly to gain anything eternal by trusting God with all our heart, soul, strength, and mind.

❖ We will take up Jesus' towel of service to meet the needs of others.

❖ We will share responsibility and authority with each other to reach our goals.

❖ We will be a ministry team to carry out God's mission in our lives.

These seven core values can become a benchmark for decisions we make as a couple. They can also serve as goals for behavior that keep our marriage "team" together.

Teams must have a reason to form and to function.

Servant leaders create teams because there is a need (related to the mission) that must be met. I talked to a pastor who was in a church that averaged seventy-two in Sunday school attendance but had forty committees! One year into his ministry there, he realized that the church had hired him to keep people on those forty committees. He was miserable. None of the committees could go away. He had to make sure every committee had at least one member on it—even if some members were on more than one committee. Mission had given way to maintenance. Committees maintain. Teams accomplish mission.

....

A TRUE TEAM IS FORMED FOR A PURPOSE,
AND THAT PURPOSE DRIVES THE TEAM
THROUGHOUT ITS EXISTENCE.

....

Too many churches are ineffective because they spend their time putting people on committees rather than building ministry teams to carry out their mission. *A true team is formed for a purpose, and that purpose drives the team throughout its existence.* This is why each ministry team must know its mission and how it relates to the overall mission of the church. That purpose drives the team throughout its existence.

No ministry team should go on without a sense of why it exists. Our church's "Kid's Celebration," our worship for three-year-olds through third graders, states its mission this way: "To *share* God's love with a contagious passion in order to *lead* children to a personal relationship with Jesus and *assist* them in building a firm foundation in God's Word." This mission guides the leaders who gather each week to guide our children in worship. It also fits perfectly with our church's mission to make disciples who know, share, and multiply Christ.

Does every team in your church know its mission as it is related to the overall mission of your church? Does every team in your business know its reason for functioning within the whole? Teams exist to score points or make goals. They cover ground and strategize to overcome an opponent. Teams with a purpose are the heart of an effective ministry or business.

A sense of togetherness prevents the leader from working alone.

Jesus multiplied his leadership by sending out his apostles (which literally means "sent ones") to do what he commissioned them to do. Servant leaders in team ministry must keep a balance between doing things themselves and encouraging others to participate. Although he may appear to have a servant's attitude, a person who does the team's work alone is not a genuine servant leader. Katzenbach and Smith give good conventional wisdom on this:

Team leaders genuinely believe that they do not have all the answers—so they do not insist on providing them. They believe they do *not* need to make all key decisions—so they do not do so. They believe they *cannot* succeed without the combined contributions of all the other members of the team to a common end—so they avoid any action that might constrain inputs or intimidate anyone on the team. Ego is *not* their predominant concern.[10]

Ego is surely not the concern of the servant leader because he humbles himself and waits for God to exalt him (see Luke 14:11).

When Jesus commissioned Peter to go and "feed [Jesus'] sheep," he did not intend for Peter to do that work alone. Henri Nouwen observed:

> But when Jesus speaks about shepherding, he does not want us to think about a brave, lonely shepherd who takes care of a large flock of obedient sheep. In many ways, he makes it clear that ministry is a communal and mutual experience.
>
> First of all, Jesus sends the twelve out in pairs (Mark 6:7). We keep forgetting that we are being sent out two by two. We cannot bring the good news on our own. We are called to proclaim the Gospel together, in community.[11]

Team ministry means going with others on mission to do what God has commissioned us to do. Individualism is not a philosophy of servant leadership.

EMPOWER WITH AUTHORITY AND PRESENCE

Servant leaders empower those on their team to reach the shared goal. Why is this important? Warren Bennis tells us why: "Basic changes take place very slowly, if at all, because those with the power generally have no knowledge, and those with the knowledge have no power."[12] Empowerment is giving power to those with the knowledge and knowledge to those with the power.

You do not empower people with a memo. Empowerment does not happen with the stroke of a pen or with a keyboard. You empower people in real time. It takes the investment of time and effort to empower someone to do the work of the team. Ken Blanchard, coauthor of *The One Minute Manager,* has captured the time it takes to empower someone in the title of his work *Empowerment Takes More than a Minute!*[13] Blanchard also teaches that one of the three keys to empowerment is "to replace the hierarchy with self-directed teams." Bill Easum teaches church leaders to empower with "self-organizing ministry teams."[14]

Jesus spent three and a half years with twelve of his closest followers to empower them to carry out his mission upon his ascension. Ministry teams are a sign of empowerment, but what does a servant leader share to empower his team? Jesus modeled the "what" of empowerment by giving his followers (1) the authority of his name and (2) the power of his presence.

The previous chapter explained how Jesus shared the authority of his name with his disciples as he shared the responsibility of his mission. Servant leaders empower members on their team with the authority of their name.

Jesus also empowered his followers with the power of his presence. Before Jesus ascended into heaven, he had given this mission to his followers: "Be my witnesses in Jerusalem, and in all Judea and Samaria, and to the ends of the earth" (Acts 1:8). The mission now has geographic markers; it has become a vision too big for those first followers to have imagined. "To the ends of the earth" was a frightening thought to these pre-Columbus followers of Jesus. Where would they find strength to go that far with the mission? The secret lies in the words that precede the mission. "But you will receive power when the Holy Spirit comes on you; and you will be my witnesses." Jesus promised the power of his presence before he shared the scope of his mission.

The Holy Spirit is the indwelling person of Jesus Christ in a disciple of Jesus. We are not left as orphans—we have his presence. We are not without power because the Spirit of Christ lives in us. Jesus empowered his followers with the power of his presence on earth and after he returned to the Father.

How can we empower the people we lead? As Jesus did, we can empower others with the authority of both our name and our presence. As pastor, I impart the authority of my position when someone can say, "The pastor said . . ." Such a statement can be powerful when the person using it is confident that power has been given to her by you.

"The pastor said . . ." can also be misused. Those who have their own agendas can use the authority of the leader to accomplish their wishes instead of those of the group. If you are a freewheeling permission giver like I tend to be, you may say something like, "Sure, that's a great idea," in the hall on a Sunday morning. By Tuesday in staff meeting, your staff may be wondering why you approved a church-wide garage sale on the same day as the twenty-four-hour prayer vigil! When you inquire how something could have happened, the reply may be, "Mrs. Smith said it was OK with you, so she put it on the calendar." Be careful how you dispense the authority of your name.

How does a person empower others with his or her presence? What did Jesus do? He spent time—long, deliberate time—with those who followed him. To instill the mission and its values in the team and to demonstrate their part in carrying out that mission, we must spend time with them. This, I believe, is why long-term ministry with one group of people is so important. If a servant leader is moving every two to three years, how much of her presence can she give to people? It takes five to seven years (unless you're Jesus!) before people even trust you enough to begin thinking about your mission, much less adjusting their lives to carry it out!

····························

IT TAKES FIVE TO SEVEN YEARS BEFORE
PEOPLE EVEN TRUST YOU ENOUGH TO
BEGIN THINKING ABOUT YOUR MISSION,
MUCH LESS ADJUSTING THEIR LIVES
TO CARRY IT OUT!

····························

To be a parent is to empower. A parent who is a servant leader will invest great amounts of time into the life of a child in order to empower the child to live as an adult. The goal of parenting is to empower a child to live out God's plan for his life. This goal requires that a parent spend time and energy to discipline and train a child in the ways of God so as an adult that child is free to live for God. Fathers are not to exasperate their children; instead, they are to "bring them up in the training and instruction of the Lord" (Eph. 6:4). Empowering children to live out God's plan for their lives is consistent with other biblical instructions to parents (Prov. 22:6).

ACCOUNT FOR THE MISSION
AND THE TEAM'S ACTIONS

Once people have been given power, they become accountable. Ken Blanchard writes, "Empowerment means you have the freedom to act; it also means you are accountable for results."[15] A characteristic of ministry teams is accountability for results related to the goal. "No group ever becomes a team until it can hold itself accountable as a team."[16] No baseball team can win the World Series until every team member makes himself accountable to the others to reach this goal. Successful team members make themselves responsible to one another to do their part.

Accountability makes team ministry possible. Accountability is the ability to account for what you have done related to a standard or expectation. Accountability keeps team members together and working toward the same goal. With it, team members can count on others to do what they say they will do. Without it, members decide on their own when, how, and if they will do their part of the work.

This concept is like mutual accountability in marriage. When I told Kim over twenty-two years ago that I would be faithful to her so we could be together until death separated us, I gave her permission to check up on me. I became accountable to her because we shared the goal of being partners for life. I have the same mutual privilege to ask her about her relationships outside our marriage. We are accountable to each other to make this marriage work in order to reach our God-given goal of marriage for life. When you make yourself responsible to others on a ministry team, you become accountable to the other members to reach your shared goal.

Accountability is part of every disciple's life. Jesus taught that every person will give an account to Holy God for his or her words and deeds. Jesus said this when he addressed a group of religious leaders who accused him of working for Satan. He said, "But I tell you that men will have to give account on the day of judgment for every careless word they have spoken" (Matt. 12:36). Paul reminded the Roman Christians that "each of us will give an account of himself to God" (Rom. 14:12). Peter encouraged his readers not to worry if pagans did not understand their lifestyle. They, too, "will have to give account to him who is ready to judge the living and the dead" (1 Pet. 4:5). Accountability to God means to give an account for your behavior while on earth. To give an account simply means to tell the truth to the person to whom you are responsible for what you have done or said.

Team accountability cannot begin until each member has a servant leader's heart. Pride will prevent a person from being accountable to anyone else. But a servant is accountable *gladly*.

What is the leader's role in accountability? Servant leaders hold the goal in place and keep the group focused on that goal. For example, if a leader recruits a team to deliver "hugs and mugs" to every first-time guest to the church, she is responsible to hold that goal/vision up to the team. She constantly reminds members of their goal as they distribute the hospitality gifts each week. If a member of the team begins to miss training and planning or does not show up to take the gifts as many times as members agreed to go out, the leader is responsible to hold that member accountable. When the goal is clear, accountability is possible.

Jesus held his disciples accountable for the true nature of his mission. Peter was blessed to acknowledge that Jesus was "the Christ, the Son of the living God" (Matt. 16:16). Jesus praised him for his insight. Peter's confession indicated that Jesus' work as leader of the mission was paying off. At least one of the Twelve had gotten the message of who he was. Jesus took Peter's confession as an opportunity to define his mission more fully. He told the group of his coming suffering and death.

Peter, as we have noted, did not want that kind of leader. He refused to accept Jesus' words about his suffering and death. He pulled Jesus aside to correct his thinking. Peter trusted his concept of the Christ rather than what his leader had just told him. Peter's ideas threatened the mission of the Messiah and the unity of the disciples.

Jesus knew the danger of Peter's attitude. A good leader corrects actions and thoughts that are "off mission." Jesus knew that his team of disciples had to be together on who Jesus was and the nature of his mission on earth. Jesus confronted Peter by saying, "Get behind me, Satan! . . . You do not have in mind the things of God, but the things of men" (Mark 8:33). Jesus called Peter Satan because the tempter had offered him the same shortcut to the kingdom (Luke 4:9-12). Jesus knew his role of Suffering Servant Messiah meant suffering and dying to complete the Father's mission of redemption. Jesus was accountable to the Father to meet this goal. As the leader, Jesus knew the need for his followers to stay committed to that same goal.

I have discovered again my need to hold our church accountable to its mission. At the time of this writing, we are building our third building in ten years. We are seeing new ministries form every month. Money and attendance are on the positive side. Yet in some members there is frustration because they don't sense that anyone knows the "why" of all this activity. As the leader, I am responsible to remind the church again why we exist. I am also accountable to ensure that all that happens is truly related to our church's mission. It's so easy for building programs and other goals to turn into their own little missions and eventually move away from the reason they were made goal sin the first place.

....

IT'S SO EASY FOR BUILDING PROGRAMS
AND OTHER GOALS TO TURN INTO THEIR
OWN LITTLE MISSIONS AND MOVE AWAY
FROM THE REASON THEY BECAME GOALS.

....

I have that same responsibility to hold my children accountable to their goals. I am fortunate that both of my daughters have put their trust in Jesus as their Lord and Savior. I, however, am responsible for their spiritual development in the home. For my youngest, that means making sure she reads Scripture more than once a week at church. So two or three mornings a week, I ask her to read portions of God's Word and tell me what they mean. Recently I asked her to read from the Sermon on the Mount. She read Jesus' teaching for us not to worry. I asked her what that passage meant. Summer likes music. She has danced or has been a cheerleader since she was three. So she answered with a rendition of Bobbie McFerrin's "Don't Worry, Be Happy." I laughed but said, "Half of that song is right, but Jesus never called us to be happy. Give it another try." She then remembered a tune from *Songs from the Loft,* "Seek First," a rendition of Matthew 6:33. "That's the message," I said, and, over our Honey Nut Cheerios and bagels, we sang the good news together.

BE A MENTOR

John Maxwell says, "There is no success without a successor."[17] I agree. I would personalize his axiom this way: "You are not a success until you have a successor." In a true team ministry the leader mentors others to continue the mission after she is gone. Servant leaders are not a success until they mentor successors to carry on the mission.

A mentor is a guide.
Mentors lead others through new terrain because they have been there before. Servant leaders show their followers what to do by doing it first; a mentor's actions weigh as heavily as words. Leaders in team ministry guide where the team is going and demonstrate the Christian lifestyle they want team members to follow.

Lynn Anderson reminds us that mentoring is an essential aspect of spiritual leadership. Anderson combines the mentor's role with that of a shepherd when he writes:

Mentor, in one sense, is another dimension of *shepherd,* but with a different emphasis. Shepherds feed, protect and care for sheep; mentors pull up alongside human beings and model behavior, values, and faith through the shared life. While the shepherd motif is the "big" model for spiritual leadership in Scripture, mentor is nonetheless essential.[18]

Spiritual leadership calls for the more mature and experienced to show others the way.

Paul was a mentor. In his first letter to the Corinthians, Paul insisted that the Christians there imitate him (4:16). We get our English word *mimic* from the Greek word Paul used. The apostle literally said, "Mimic me!" Following a mentor is a form of mimicking someone. Coaches have athletes do it all the time. A coach will say, "Do it this way." The athlete then mimics the coach's instructions—sometimes again and again until she gets it right.

One test of whether or not you are a mentor of the faith is to ask yourself, "Could I, like Paul, insist that an individual and/or a group of people mimic my behavior for a week in order to learn how to follow Jesus?" What kind of Christians would you produce if the only way they learned how to walk with the Lord was by following you around and mimicking your actions? The answers to those questions may tell why or why not your marriage, home, business, or church is not growing in the Lord. As Mary Kay Ash teaches, "The speed of the leader is the speed of the gang."[19]

Mike is one of our pastoral interns. He and his wife came to our church seven years ago. Since their coming, God has confirmed the call to full-time mission in Mike and Karen's life. As the church has affirmed that calling, we have licensed and ordained Mike. We have invested in his seminary training. Mike has graduated from seminary and is looking for a full-time staff position while continuing to serve our church as director of assimilation and adult Bible studies.

I have been blessed to be one of Mike's mentors. Officially, I am his pastor and field-experience supervisor. Unofficially, I am fortunate to be a guide. Mike is the one who teaches our membership workshop while I preach on Sunday mornings. He is the one I send to teach the principles in this book when I cannot. Mike embodies the mission of Legacy Drive Baptist Church. He has helped design and implement all that applies to assimilating new members into the life of this church. Mike is my protégé. Servant leaders mentor others to join them in team ministry. Mentoring is how the work of Christ passes on from one generation of followers to the next.

Jesus mentored his disciples by teaching them.

Matthew 5; 6; and 7 record Jesus' "design for discipleship." He taught how kingdom people live. Jesus taught his disciples about humility, greatness, and being first in line. He turned everyday situations into instant classrooms. He was always looking beyond the obvious words and actions to the thoughts, motivations, and beliefs behind them. Jesus didn't merely give his followers information; he led them into seeing life in a different way. He took them deeper—and broader. He taught through stories, parables, and simple objects that were familiar. I think it's safe to say that Jesus viewed all of life from the position of being a teacher, looking for opportunities to illumine the thinking and stimulate the faith of his followers.

Jesus also mentored his followers by demonstrating the power of God in their lives.

When the disciples thought there was no way to feed a crowd that had followed them all day, Jesus asked God to provide enough food from a boy's lunch to feed the five thousand

(Mark 6:32-44). Jesus didn't use power foolishly or to show off in front of friend or foe. There was always a purpose behind Jesus' use of power. When the disciples wanted him to use his power to call down fire on a town, he refused. Even through the way he used his power, Jesus was building the faith and understanding of the disciples.

Jesus mentored by modeling a life of prayer for his followers.

Luke 6:12 tells us that he prayed all night before choosing the Twelve. We have seen how Jesus equipped his followers when they asked him to teach them to pray (Luke 11:1-4). They usually knew where to find him praying—evidence that Jesus' prayer life was a constant. Many times he talked with his heavenly Father in front of his followers. These people had never imagined calling God "Father," but Jesus helped them grow accustomed to the idea.

AN OLD TESTAMENT LESSON IN MENTORING

The principles of mentoring and delegation are not new. After the Exodus, Moses was responsible for leading the children of Israel to the Promised Land. One responsibility was to make decisions regarding disputes between people. The only problem was that there were hundreds of thousands of people! Jethro was Moses' father-in-law. He helped Moses by teaching him how to multiply his leadership through mentoring rather than doing all the work alone. Carl George calls Jethro's insights "The Jethro Principle."[20]

When Jethro told Moses he was going to wear himself out unless he multiplied his leadership, he told Moses he had three responsibilities as a leader (Exod. 18:19-20). The first was to "be the people's representative before God and bring their disputes to him." Moses' first responsibility as leader was a priestly one.

He knew God and his people as he carried their needs before God. Spiritual leaders represent their followers to God. Calvin Miller says that God's leaders need to "talk more to God about people, than to people about their problems."[21] Empowering leadership begins when the leader is empowered by God.

Jethro's second injunction to Moses as an empowering leader was to "teach them the decrees and laws." Leaders instruct followers in core values and boundaries of behavior. Moses was to teach the people the ways of God. He had to define and articulate God's plan for the people before he could enlist others to make decisions with him.

Finally, Jethro said, "show them the way to live and the duties they are to perform." Moses not only taught God's ways, he modeled God's ways. Those he would appoint to judge the people had to have a pattern for how they were to act. That model came from the leader.

....

LEADERS WEAR OUT THEIR FOLLOWERS AND THEMSELVES WHEN THEY TRY TO LEAD ALONE.

....

Leaders wear out their followers and themselves when they try to lead alone. Stephen Covey observes, "People and organizations don't grow much without delegation and completed staff work, because they are confined to the capacities of the boss and reflect both personal strengths and weaknesses."[22] Too many church leaders suffer burnout because they think they are the only ones who can do the job. Owning responsibility does not mean you alone can do the task. Servant leaders know they are most effective when they trust others to work with them. Good leaders mentor and empower capable people to help them do the job.

THE LEADER NEEDS A MENTOR TOO

As a servant leader, you are a mentor to those you have called
to be on your team. But you also need a mentor. A servant
leader humbly acknowledges his need for someone who has
been down the road to be a guide through the minefields.
Writing for Promise Keepers, Howard Hendricks has recom-
mended that every man have three individuals in his life: "You
need a Paul. You need a Barnabas. You need a Timothy."[23]
While Promise Keepers is a ministry to men by men, this principle applies to everyone in the body of Christ. Paul advises
Titus to have the older women teach the younger women the
ways of God (Titus 2:3-5).

Hendricks encourages each believer to have a Paul in his
life because "you need someone who's been down the road."
Every believer needs a Barnabas because you need someone
"who loves you but is not impressed by you." (That's my wife!
She loves me but is not impressed by all that I do. I need someone like her in my life, and I am blessed that she is my "Barnabas.") You also need a Timothy "into whose life you are
building."

I would summarize Hendricks's points this way: You need
a pastor, a partner, and a protégé. A pastor (not necessarily
the paid professional kind) will show you down the road. Your
partner will love you but not be impressed by anything other
than authentic relationship. Having a protégé means you are
passing on the mission God has placed on your life.

Mentoring is how servant leaders prepare the next generation of leaders for service. Unless there are future leaders, there
is no future.

You have not reached the goal of servant leadership until
you have built a ministry team around you. You will carry out
Christ's mission most effectively through ministry teams.

FOR STUDY AND REFLECTION

- Jesus built a leadership team. Based on your study of this chapter and Jesus' life, why do you believe he did that?

- Why, according to the author, is leading a team the highest expression of servant leadership?

- List the four steps to build a team. T_____ E_____ A_____ M_____.

- List the names of those on the team you lead.

- List two ways you can create a sense of togetherness on your team.

- List two ways you can empower with authority and presence.

- List two ways you can account for the mission and the team's actions.

- List two things you can do this week to be a mentor for someone on your team.

- Who is your "pastor"? Who is your "partner"? Who is your "protégé"?

- Summarize your understanding of the seventh principle of servant leadership. Write three ways you can build your team this week.

Endnotes for Principle #7

1. We were surprised at the rapid growth of this ministry until we checked the demographic data and discovered there were over fifteen hundred internationals within a two-mile radius of our church! Our strategic-planning teams had overlooked this opportunity. God had not.

2. Jon R. Katzenbach and Douglas K. Smith, *The Wisdom of Teams: Creating the High-Performance Organization* (Boston: Harvard Business School Press, 1993), 45.

3. Ibid., 15.

4. John Maxwell, *Developing the Leaders around You* (Nashville: Nelson, 1995), 135.

5. Robert K. Greenleaf, *Servant Leadership* (Mahwah, N.J.: Paulist, 1977), 67.

6. C. Gene Wilkes, *Jesus on Leadership* (Nashville: LifeWay Press, 1990), 103-121.

7. William Mitchell, *The Power of Positive Parenting* (Grand Rapids: Revell, 1989). The POPS Web site is www.pops.com.

8. Peter Drucker, *Managing the Non-Profit Organization* (New York: HarperCollins, 1990), 152–53.

9. Stephen R. Covey, *Principle-Centered Leadership* (New York: Simon and Schuster, 1992), 246.

10. Katzenbach and Smith, *The Wisdom of Teams: Creating the High-Performance Organization,* 131.

11. Henri J. M. Nouwen, *In the Name of Jesus: Reflections on Christian Leadership* (New York: Crossroad, 1989), 40.

12. Warren Bennis, *Why Leaders Can't Lead* (San Francisco: Jossey-Bass, 1989), 30.

13. Ken Blanchard, John P. Carlos and Allan Randolph, *Empowerment Takes More Than a Minute* (San Francisco: Berrett-Koehler, 1996).

14. Bill Easum, *Sacred Cows Make Gourmet Burgers* (Nashville: Abingdon, 1995), 113–130.

15. Blanchard, Carlos, and Randolph, *Empowerment Takes More than a Minute,* 90.

16. Katzenbach and Smith, *The Wisdom of Teams: Creating the High-Performance Organization,* 60.

17. Maxwell, *Developing the Leaders around You,* 11.

18. Lynn Anderson, *They Smell Like Sheep* (West Monroe, La.: Howard, 1997), 49.

19. Mary Kay Ash, *Mary Kay on People Management* (New York: Warner, 1984), 65.

20. Carl F. George, *Prepare Your Church for the Future* (Grand Rapids: Revell, 1991), 121–5. Larry Smith, one of my deacon officers who graduated from West Point, showed me Jethro's advice in the Army's "Leadership in Organizations" (1981 ed., 18–1).

21. Calvin Miller, *The Empowered Leader* (Nashville: Broadman & Holman, 1995), 84.

22. Covey, *Principle-Centered Leadership,* 237.

23. Howard Hendricks, *Seven Promises of a Promise Keeper* (Colorado Springs: Focus on the Family, 1994), 53–4.

EPILOGUE

YOU HAVE completed another book on leadership, and you may be where I am every time I finish reading someone else's thoughts: I wonder why I didn't see those things when I read about Jesus, or I ask, "What can I take with me?" or, "What in here can I do today to change how I lead others?" You may also compare the contents of this book with others you have read on the subject, wondering what is timeless and what is trendy. Whatever your response, my hope is that I have put you face-to-face with Jesus, and you must once again decide if you will follow him.

Someone much wiser than me has said that leadership cannot be taught; it must be learned. I agree. My prayer is that this introduction to how Jesus led will help you as you learn to lead. Everything on these pages was learned in the classroom of experiences; some exhilarating, some numbingly painful. Your best lessons of leadership will come from everyday events and decisions. But don't let experience alone teach you. You need a Mentor. I believe Jesus, the Christ, is your best guide for learning to lead among God's people. I invite you to allow Jesus to be your model and source of understanding of how to lead others.

My prayer is that this culture (and churches!) will become curious about this strange group that leads dressed like servants and acting like slaves. And, in their curiosity, they will come to trust the Servant Leader who taught us to lead that way.

C. Gene Wilkes
April 1998

CONTEMPORARY
IDEAS ABOUT
SERVANT LEADERSHIP

IN 1970, Robert Greenleaf, then an executive in the communications industry, announced to the world that a "new moral principle" was emerging in society. He wrote that people will not accept the authority of existing institutions. *"Rather, they will freely respond only to individuals who are chosen as leaders because they are proven and trusted as servants. . . . In the* future, the only truly viable institutions will be those that are predominately servant-led."[1] What is a servant leader? Greenleaf wrote, "The servant-leader is servant first. . . . It begins with the natural feeling that one wants to serve, to serve first. Then conscious choice brings one to aspire to lead."[2]

Greenleaf applied his definition of the servant as leader to institutions and their trustees. He argued that caring for others makes for a good society. He observed that most caring had been mediated to institutions and away from individuals. Greenleaf reasoned that institutions serve society best when they "raise the performance as servant of as many institutions as possible by new voluntary regenerative forces initiated within them by committed individuals, servants."[3] The servant as leader would foster care through society's institutions. Greenleaf applied this model of leadership to business, schools, churches, and seminaries.

Greenleaf's ideas have proven to be prophetic. Several contemporary observers of our leadership climate call for service as a core motivation and characteristic of leaders. Greenleaf's concepts remain vital because they are practical and translate into the daily responsibilities of those who lead. While his principles are valid to our discussion, they are not complete. Greenleaf, I believe, minimized the one who modeled servant leadership ultimately: Jesus. Greenleaf appreciated Jesus. He wrote that Jesus was "a leader in the fullest meaning of the word."[4] He acknowledged Jesus' skill of "withdrawal" to diffuse a tense situation with the woman caught in adultery.[5] However, he criticized Jesus' decision to coerce the money changers from the temple rather than build a consensus with the group.[6] For Greenleaf, Jesus is a *historical* model of servant leadership. I, on the other hand, believe Jesus is *the best model* for servant leadership.

I noted earlier that Greenleaf wrote that servant leadership begins "with the natural feeling that one wants to serve, to serve first. Then conscious choice brings one to aspire to lead." A natural feeling to serve precedes a choice to lead, according to Greenleaf. That is a lofty insight about people. I, on the other hand, have observed that most people choose to lead long before they choose to serve. I submit that our "natural feeling" is self-promotion or self-protection, not service to others. Our attitude, if we are honest, is that we would rather have others serve us than serve others ourselves. We say inside, *You can have the seats in the balcony. I'll sit down front, thank you.* I believe we see so few servant leaders because very few have a "natural feeling" to serve! Only a sense of call to mission and Christ's presence can guide a person's heart to choose service to others first.

Greenleaf's concepts remain vital to the discussion of servant leadership. They should play a vital role in how leaders pattern their lives. I believe people really do want the idea of the "servant as leader" to work. Down deep we know it is better to serve than to be served. We also know how hard it is to put others first. How, then, does this change come about? I am convinced that Christ alone empowers a self-centered person to become an other-serving person. This is why I am convinced that only one who is in relationship with Jesus Christ can truly become a servant leader.

Other contemporary writers have called leaders in the marketplace to become servant leaders. Max DePree draws this modern picture of this kind of leadership:

> A jazz band is an expression of servant leadership. The leader of a jazz band has the beautiful opportunity to draw the best out of the other musicians. We have much to learn from jazz-band leaders, for jazz, like leadership, combines the unpredictability of the future with the gifts of individuals.[7]

DePree paints servant leadership as a jazz-band leader—not a model taught in too many business schools or seminaries! Corporate and church leaders struggle to translate his example into their lives. When most organizations sound more like cacophony than symphony, a jazz band seems out of the question! DePree, on the other hand, has painted the reality that servant leadership begins as the leader knows those who are in her band and who spend hours together creating improvisations for the future.

Stephen Covey has observed that "principle-centered leaders" are service-oriented. He notes: "Those striving to be principle-centered see life as a mission, not as a career. Their nurturing sources have armed and prepared them for service. In effect, every morning they 'yoke up' and put on the harness of service, thinking of others."[8] Covey's call away from personality-centered leadership has created a climate for examining again the power of the servant-leadership model in everyday life.

Calvin Miller guides us to King David as a model of servant leadership.[9] Miller notes that "The spiritual life of a leader gathers itself around a single powerful idea—servanthood. . . . The spiritual leader is one who yields to God for his or her best work."[10] This "yielding to God" is the foundation of leading like Jesus. Leaders in the kingdom of God serve God and those given to them to lead.

Laurie Beth Jones, author of *Jesus, CEO,* presents Jesus as an ancient figure from whom we can learn how to be visionary leaders. Ms. Jones has discovered seventy-five concepts Jesus can teach us about leadership. She notes the servant aspect of Jesus' leadership style:

> Jesus, the leader, served his people. Most religions teach that we are put here to serve God; yet, in Jesus, God is offering to serve us. Some people are shocked at the inference that God serves us. Yet this man who represented God—who was imbued with all the power of God—walked up to people and asked, "How can I help you?"[11]

Jones portrays Jesus as a leader who serves those who follow him. She has brought Jesus to the forefront as an example twentieth-century leaders can follow. This pithy book introduces the person of Jesus to those who may not know him. I agree with Jones that Jesus can teach us much about leadership. The popularity of this book tells the story that modern men and women still accept Jesus as a model of leadership.

As I observed with Greenleaf, I believe Jones has not presented the full impact of who Jesus can be in the life of a leader. Her valuable work opens the door for postmoderns to consider Jesus as an ancient authority who has something to offer us at the end of this millennium. Yet, while Jesus was a leader of a movement and has much to teach us from a human perspective, Jesus was surely the Son of God, who came to carry out the eternal mission of bringing salvation to all people. We are changed by Jesus not because we observe him but because we dare to follow him.

These books and others signal a turn from leadership based on self-interest to leadership based on service to those whom the leader leads. These who observe leaders recognize the importance of a service element in the character of those who lead. This turn toward leaders who serve makes Jesus' model of leadership even more viable in today's marketplace of ideas.

Endnotes for Contemporary Ideas about Servant Leadership

1. Greenleaf, Robert K. *Servant Leadership,* (Mahwah, N.J.: Paulist Press, 1977), 10. Italics mine.

2. Ibid., 13. This definition and other interests of Greenleaf can be found on the Robert K. Greenleaf Center for Servant-Leadership Web site www.greenleaf.org.

3. Quoted in Frick, Don M. and Spears, Larry C., editors. *On Becoming a Servant-Leader* (San Francisco: Jossey-Bass, 1996), 5.

4. Ibid., 324.

5. Ibid., 325.

6. Ibid., 140.

7. Max DePree, *Leadership Jazz* (New York: Currency/Doubleday, 1992), 9.

8. Stephen Covey, *Principle-Centered Leadership* (New York: Simon and Schuster, 1992), 34.

9. Calvin Miller, *The Empowered Leader* (Broadman & Holman, 1995).

10. *Ibid.,* 14.

11. Laurie Beth Jones, *Jesus, CEO: Using Ancient Wisdom for Visionary Leadership* (New York: Hyperion, 1995), 250–51.

BIBLIOGRAPHY

Books Related to Leadership

Ash, Mary Kay. *Mary Kay on People Management.* New York: Warner, 1984.

Barker, Joel Arthur. *Future Edge: Discovering the New Rules of Success.* New York: William Morrow and Company, 1992.

Bennis, Warren. *On Becoming a Leader.* Reading, Mass.: Addison-Wesley Publishing, 1994.

———. *Why Leaders Can't Lead.* San Francisco: Jossey-Bass, 1990.

Blanchard, Ken, John P. Carlos, and Allan Randolph. *Empowerment Takes More Than a Minute.* San Francisco: Berrett-Koehler. 1996.

Block, Peter. *Stewardship, Choosing Service over Self-Interest.* San Francisco: Berrett-Koehler, 1993.

Bracey, Hyler, Jack Rosenblum, Aubrey Sanford, and Roy Trueblood. *Managing from the Heart.* New York: Dell, 1990.

Burns, James MacGregor. *Leadership.* New York: Harper & Row, 1978.

Collins, James C., and Jerry I. Porras. *Built to Last: Successful Habits of Visionary Companies.* New York: Harper Business, 1997.

Covey, Stephen R. *Principle-Centered Leadership: Strategies for Personal and Professional Effectiveness.* New York: Simon & Schuster, 1992.

DePree, Max. *Leadership Is an Art.* New York: Doubleday, 1989.

———. *Leadership Jazz.* New York: Doubleday, 1992.

———. *Leading without Power.* San Francisco: Jossey-Bass, 1997.

Drucker, Peter. *Managing the Non-Profit Organization.* New York: Harper Business, 1992.

Gardner, Howard. *Leading Minds: An Anatomy of Leadership.* New York: Basic, 1996.

Greenleaf, Robert K. *On Becoming a Servant Leader,* edited by Don M. Frick and Larry C. Spears. San Francisco: Jossey-Bass, 1996.

———. *Servant Leadership.* Mahwah, N.J.: Paulist, 1977.

Hayward, Steven F. *Churchill on Leadership.* Rocklin, Calif.: Prima, 1997.

Jones, Laurie Beth. *Jesus, CEO: Using Ancient Wisdom for Visionary Leadership.* New York: Hyperion, 1995.

Katzenbach, Jon R., and Douglas K. Smith. *The Wisdom of Teams: Creating the High-Performance Organization.* Boston: Harvard Business School Press, 1993.

Kostner, Jaclyn. *Virtual Leadership: Secrets from the Round Table for the Multi-Site Manager.* New York: Warner, 1996.

Kouzes, James M., and Barry Z. Posner. *The Leadership Challenge.* San Francisco: Jossey-Bass, 1987.

Nanus, Bert. *Visionary Leadership.* San Francisco: Jossey-Bass, 1992.

Peters, Tom. *Thriving on Chaos,* Perennial Library ed. New York: Harper & Row, Perennial Library Edition, 1987.

Phillips, Donald T. *Lincoln on Leadership.* New York: Warner, 1993.

Senge, Peter. *The Fifth Discipline: The Art and Practice of the Learning Organization.* New York: Doubleday, 1990.

Smith, Douglas K. "The Following Part of Leading." *The Leader of the Future.* ed. by Frances Hesselbein, Marshall Goldsmith, and Richard Beckhard. San Francisco: Jossey-Bass, 1997.

Books Related to Church and Christian Leadership

Anderson, Leith. *A Church for the Twenty-First Century.* Minneapolis: Bethany, 1992.

Anderson, Lynn. *They Smell Like Sheep.* West Monroe, La.: Howard, 1997.

Barna, George. *The Power of Vision.* Ventura, Calif.: Regal, 1992.

Callahan, Kennon. *Effective Church Leadership.* New York: Harper & Row, 1990.

Dale, Robert D. *Leading Edge: Leadership Strategies from the New Testament.* Nashville: Abingdon, 1996.

Easum, William M. *Sacred Cows Make Gourmet Burgers.* Nashville: Abingdon, 1995.

Easum, William M., and Thomas G. Bandy. *Growing Spiritual Redwoods.* Nashville: Abingdon, 1997.

George, Carl F. *Prepare Your Church for the Future.* Grand Rapids: Revell, 1991.

Hemphill, Ken. *The Antioch Effect.* Nashville: Broadman & Holman, 1994.

Maxwell, John. *Developing the Leaders around You.* Nashville: Nelson, 1995.

Miller, Calvin. *The Empowered Leader*. Nashville: Broadman & Holman, 1995.

Murren, Doug. *Leadershift*. Ventura, Calif.: Regal, 1994.

Nouwen, Henri J. M. *In the Name of Jesus: Reflections on Christian Leadership*. New York: Crossroad, 1989.

Sanders, Oswald. *Spiritual Leadership*. Chicago: Moody Press, 1967.

Stowell, Joseph M. *Shepherding the Church into the Twenty-First Century*. Colorado Springs: Victor, 1994.

Warren, Rick. *The Purpose-Driven Church*. Grand Rapids: Zondervan, 1995.

Weems, Lovett H., Jr., *Church Leadership*. Nashville: Abingdon, 1993.

Wilkes, C. Gene. *Jesus on Leadership: Becoming a Servant Leader*. Nashville: LifeWay Press, 1996.

Books Related to the Christian's Life

Blackaby, Henry, and Claude King, *Experiencing God*. Nashville: Broadman & Holman, 1990.

Blanchard, Ken. *We Are the Beloved*. Grand Rapids: Zondervan, 1994.

Boone, Wellington. *Breaking Through*. Nashville: Broadman & Holman, 1995.

Buford, Bob. *Game Plan*. Grand Rapids: Zondervan, 1997.

———. *Halftime*. Grand Rapids: Zondervan, 1994.

Carter, Jimmy. *Living Faith*. New York: Times Books, 1996.

Foster, Richard J. *Celebration of Discipline*. New York: HarperCollins, 1988, Revised and expanded edition.

Hendricks, Howard. *Seven Promises of a Promise Keeper*. Colorado Springs: Focus on the Family, 1994.

Hybels, Bill, and Rob Wilkins. *Descending into Greatness*. Grand Rapids: Zondervan, 1993.

LaHaye, Tim. *Spirit-Controlled Temperament*. Wheaton, Ill.: Tyndale House, 1966.

Manning, Brennan. *The Signature of Jesus*. Sisters, Oreg.: Multnomah, 1996.

McNeill, Donald P., Douglas A. Morrison, and Henri J. M. Nouwen. *Compassion: A Reflection on the Christian Life*. New York: Doubleday, 1983.

Mitchell, William, and Charles Paul Conn. *The Power of Positive Parenting.* Grand Rapids: Revell, 1989.

Mitchell, William, and Michael A. Mitchell. *Building Strong Families.* Nashville: Broadman & Holman, 1997.

Schuller, Robert H. *Prayer: My Soul's Adventure with God.* Nashville: Nelson, 1995.

Shank, Bob. *Total Life Management.* Sisters, Oreg.: Multnomah, 1990.

Smalley, Gary. *Making Love Last Forever.* Waco, Tex.: Word, 1996.

Smalley, Gary, and John Trent. *The Two Sides of Love.* Colorado Springs: Focus on the Family, 1990.

Trent, John. *LifeMapping.* Colorado Springs: Focus on the Family, 1994.

Voges, Ken, and Ron Braund. *Understanding How Others Misunderstand You.* Chicago: Moody Press, 1990.

Audio/Video Resources

Card, Michael. "The Basin and The Towel," on *Poiema* (CD) Brentwood, Tenn.: The Sparrow Corporation, 1994.

Bolz, Ray. "I've Come to Serve," on *The Concert of a Lifetime* (Video) Nashville: Word Music, 1995.

ABOUT THE AUTHOR

 GENE WILKES is the pastor of Legacy Drive Baptist Church in Plano, Texas, where he has served since 1987. Legacy Drive is known for its innovative methods of ministry and its contemporary worship style.

Gene is author of the workbook *Jesus on Leadership: Becoming a Servant Leader* and the leader's guide *Jesus on Leadership: Developing Servant Leaders* (LifeWay Press). He is a national conference leader on the topics of leadership and lay mobilization and has taught at the doctor of ministry level on the topics of church leadership and innovative ministry. Currently, he serves on the board of advisors for the Texas Baptist Leadership Center. Gene has written for such publications as *Worship Leader* and *Growing Churches,* and wrote the devotionals for *The Ultimate Youth Choir Book 1 & 2,* published by Word Music.

Gene earned his bachelor of arts degree from Baylor University in Waco, Texas, and his master of divinity and doctorate of philosophy degrees from Southwestern Baptist Theological Seminary in Fort Worth, Texas.

He is married to Kim McHan Wilkes, and they have two daughters.

BECOMING A SERVANT LEADER...
PUTTING PRINCIPLES INTO PRACTICE

SOMETIMES it's not enough just to have a heart for servant leadership. You need help. And you'll find it with the LifeWay edition of *Jesus on Leadership.*

This unique five-week study teaches the practical application of the principles you've been reading about in *Jesus on Leadership: Discovering the Secrets of Servant Leadership from the Life of Christ.* What's more, it gives you the tools you need to help you follow Jesus' example of servant leadership.

Jesus on Leadership: Becoming a Servant Leader Workbook
At the core of this small-group Bible study is the *Jesus on Leadership: Becoming a Servant Leader* workbook. With its easy, five-lessons-per-week format, the workbook lets you interact directly with the content, principles, and message of *Jesus on Leadership.*

Plus, it includes the spiritual-gifts inventory, the DISC relational survey, and the S.E.R.V.E. profile discussed in *Jesus on Leadership.* Participants can work through each exercise on their own time and at their own pace—then each week, meet with others in the group to share insights about themselves and discover how God has prepared them to serve and equip others for team ministry.

Jesus on Leadership: Developing Servant Leaders Kit
To facilitate this unique small-group study, we've also created the *Jesus on Leadership Kit.* Each kit includes a leader's guide to facilitate the six

small-group sessions (complete with masters for overhead transparencies or handouts); a six-part videotape (discussion starters for each session plus help for the facilitator by Gene Wilkes); a reproducible audiocassette summary narrated by Gene Wilkes; a PC computer diskette; and a sample workbook.

From pastors to potential leaders, this is an excellent resource for developing and applying the concept of servant leadership in the church. Additional workbooks and leader's guides are available separately.

When desire alone is not enough, when you need direction—that's when you need *Jesus on Leadership: Becoming a Servant Leader.*

Jesus on Leadership: Developing Servant Leaders Kit
08054-9351-4 $59.95

Jesus on Leadership: Becoming a Servant Leader Workbook
0-7673-9855-6 $9.95

Jesus on Leadership: Leader's Guide
0-7673-9854-8 $6.95

For more information, or to place an order, call 1-800-458-2772; or visit the Baptist Book Store or LifeWay Christian Store serving you. Prices subject to change. Final order total will include applicable taxes and shipping/handling charges.